A PASSIO[N]
FLYING

Exciting Stories of a Boeing Test Pilot

Ambassador-Emerald • Int'l

Getting the Word Around

MARVIN MICHAEL

Foreword By U.S. Congressman Rod Chandler

D1760968

A Passion for Flying: Exciting Stories of a Boeing Test Pilot
Copyright ©1999 Marvin Michael·

All Rights Reserved

No part of this book may be reproduced, stored in a retrieval system, or
transmitted in any form or by any means—electronic, mechanical,
photocopy,recording,or otherwise—without written permission of the publisher,
except for brief quotation in written reviews.

Published by

Ambassador-Emerald International

1 Chick Springs Road, Suite 203
Greenville, SC 29609 USA

and

Ambassador Productions
16 Hillview Avenue
Belfast, Northern Ireland
BT5 6JR

Cover design © 1999 Samuel Laterza
Cover Photography :background © 1999 by Corel Corporation

This book is dedicated with great respect and admiration to the memory of Edmund T. Allen, the greatest of test pilots, who served as a beloved mentor, and who gave me a motto to live by: The grand struggle against big odds toward an achievement.

ACKNOWLEDGMENTS

I hereby express my gratitude to my wife and children, whose loving support enabled me to follow my dream. I am grateful for the help of Peggy Anderson, Ellie Bator, Elaine Wright Colvin and Mary Sikkema. My thanks go also to all of those associates who played an important role in my career as a test pilot at Boeing. I am grateful to The Boeing Company for its outstanding leadership in worldwide aviation, and for the opportunity it gave me to enjoy a challenging and rewarding career in that field. My appreciation goes also to Margaret Marshall, for her excellent editorial assistance.

CONTENTS

FOREWORD
by Rod Chandler
Congress of the United States
House of Representatives

"Aviation" is as much an element of my blood as platelets and corpuscles. From my first glimpse of a DC-3 or a Piper Cub to the day I soloed, I always wanted to be a pilot. Some of us are simply infected with an unexplainable but overwhelming enthusiasm for flying.

That is why I admire and want to know more about men like Marvin Michael. He not only is a fellow pilot, but he is an aviation pioneer. Marvin worked alongside many of the great talents in aircraft design and testing. Like so many of them, he has a story to tell of excitement, uncertainty and, due to world war, extreme urgency.

The people with whom Marvin worked are heroes too. They put their lives on the line to assure the safety and reliability of America's war birds. Their stories are fascinating and inspirational.

In his book, *A Passion for Flying*, Marvin takes the reader onto the flight deck of untried airplanes. He introduces the "characters" who, along with him, took the risk of flying planes which contained undetected flaws. He tells of crashes which led to life saving design changes. He recounts the tragedy of lost lives and the wonder of surviving and flying another day.

For an "airplane nut" like me, Marvin Michael's story is a must-read. I know it will also be an inspiration to today's young people who learn that Marvin was, at one time, just like them—trying to find a place in aviation.

The history of aviation is not just a story of aluminum skins and radial engines. It is much more the story of people who had blue sky, clouds and Avgas in their veins and became the "Eagles" of a brave new field.

Congratulations to Marvin for his life's work and his devotion to telling a story which we all deserve to know.

Chapter One

A Dream Takes Wings

"Airplane! Airplane!" my brother yelled. Even as I dashed outside, I heard the sputter over our house. In 1926, airplanes were such an infrequent sight in the small town of Garden City, Kansas, that the beholder was duty-bound to alert the neighborhood. The plane my brother announced gradually descended and then appeared to land nearby.

Since the age of 10, when I saw my first airplane, I had been obsessed with man's ability to take to the air. I *knew* I would have my own airplane when I grew up, and I imagined what it would be like to fly a plane and look down on the earth from a great height. Now, at 14, I read everything I could on the subject and was determined to find some way to get myself airborne in the near future (a fairly ambitious goal for a minister's son in a small Kansas town). Today might very well be the day! The nearby landing of the biplane seemed to be a part of my grand scheme. Knowing that these barnstorming pilots often took passengers for a brief ride at a minimal charge, I ran back in the house and robbed my piggybank of three dollars in coins.

I hopped on my bike and headed toward the area where I thought the plane had landed. The Kansas summer sun plastered my shirt to my back as I pedaled furiously along the hard dirt road for a distance of about two miles. The plane had put down in a grassy pasture, but just as I arrived it taxied out to takeoff. I threw my bike down, climbed through a wire fence and raced to the crowd of noisy onlookers. There were men in overalls, women in flowery cotton dresses, a group of young boys, and barking dogs.

I grabbed a bystander's arm and yelled above the noise of the plane: "Is he leaving?"

"Naw—he's giving rides."

"Do you know how much it costs?"

"Two-fifty. See the man selling tickets over there?"

I grinned broadly. This was my lucky day all right— I had three dollars! I muscled my way through the crowd. The ticket seller, in Levis and a flamboyant striped shirt, was in his twenties.

"How much is a ride?" I asked, just to make sure.

"Two-fifty." I counted out the coins and took the ticket.

The airplane wobbled as it came back in for a landing. From my avid reading, I recognized it as a Lincoln Standard biplane. When it came to a stop I ran across the field prepared to climb aboard, but was disappointed to find there was another passenger load ahead of me. I watched their takeoff with interest, and although it was probably only a fifteen minute flight, it seemed much longer than that.

At last the plane landed. The pilot taxied up, jazzed the throttle and swung the plane around. As they came closer I could see him in the rear cockpit. He pushed his goggles up on his forehead and waited as the four intrepid flyers disembarked, looking thrilled with their experience.

The next four of us then stepped onto the lower wing and entered the forward cockpit. I seated myself on a leather-covered bench. Two of us sat in the rear, facing the other two passengers. My seatmate and I shared a wide safety belt. I was so excited I could hardly sit still.

Dust flew as the pilot advanced the throttle and the plane moved forward. Once clear of the crowd, he opened the throttle and we slowly accelerated. He lifted the tail and I looked out the side as the green grass rushed by. Suddenly the bouncing over rough ground ceased and we were in the air. I couldn't believe we were really flying. As the earth dropped away the wind blew in and made my eyes water. We passed over farmhouses and barns as we gradually gained altitude. I wanted to holler "Whoopee!" but was afraid the other passengers would think I was silly. The plane seemed to hang motionless, and in that moment I said to myself, "I'm gonna learn to fly just as soon as I can."

When we stopped climbing and leveled off at 70 miles per hour, I was surprised by the sensation that we were barely creeping. I was amazed that things on the ground were so tiny. Haystacks appeared to be loaves of bread. A car moving down the road looked like a toy. Flying over town, I was thrilled to recognize my house, the high school and many other buildings, even though I saw mostly roofs. The staccato roar of the engine was music to my ears. The exhaust fumes were more fragrant to me than new-mown hay.

All too soon we returned for a landing. As the pilot throttled back and we descended, the engine purred softly and my ears popped. Buildings and trees flashed by and we touched down gently on the sod, then bounced along the rough field. We turned around, slowly taxied to a stop and I climbed out, beaming with satisfaction. I wanted to run away with the pilot!

In a state of euphoria I pedaled home and glowingly described the flight to my family. I added some finishing touches to the model airplane on which I'd been working when I heard my brother's clarion call. Now I suddenly realized that miniature balsa wood planes were not going to satisfy my needs for much longer. I had found my wings.

Shortly after World War I there was a popular song called "How Ya' Gonna Keep 'em Down on the Farm, After They've Seen Paree?" It was obvious to me now that life on a Kansas farm was not at all what fate had in store for me.

* * * *

When Charles Lindbergh made his famous non-stop solo flight from New York to Paris in 1927, I saved every picture and news clipping I could find. He was my hero.

"Dad, can't we listen to the radio news about Lindbergh?"

My father was listening to another program, but he sensed how important this was to me. "All right, son" he said, tuning in another station.

I'd been devouring the few aviation magazines that were available, but now I browsed through the newsstands constantly, looking for anything about Lindbergh. If only I could be like Lindy!

A well-publicized newspaper picture of Lindbergh in his leather helmet, goggles perched on his forehead, captured my attention. I sent off to Wichita for a helmet and goggles which were advertised in an aviation magazine. They were expensive, but I had to have them. When they arrived, I struck a pose just like Lindbergh, and Dad took my picture with his box camera. I was one of the young fellows in whom the transatlantic flight inspired the determination to become an airmail pilot just like Lindy.

Lindbergh's feat greatly stimulated interest in aviation. Pilots could not be expected to depend forever upon a handy pasture in which to land. Airports, although primitive, began to appear throughout the nation. From small town to metropolis, city fathers saw the writing in the sky and prepared to enter the air age. My home town was not to be left out. In 1928 the headline read: "GARDEN CITY AIRPORT IS NOW ASSURED." The article read: "On Saturday, January 14, Charles Eggen, chairman of the Aviation Committee of the Chamber of Commerce, signed a contract for a five-year lease on eighty acres, two and three quarter miles east of the city. The new airport site is ideally located for all-year-round flying conditions..." There wasn't much effort needed to build an airport in those days. The landing field was grass. (There still are grass airports. In my state of Washington, a few miles west of Snoqualmie Pass in the Cascade Mountains there is an FAA emergency landing field which is grass.)

Carl Gibson built a hangar in Garden City and set up shop with his three-passenger Travel Air biplane. He gave rides and flying lessons.

Flight maps were unheard of. Barnstormers drew lines on service station road maps to use in navigation.

Years later, government flight charts showed railroads, power lines, rivers and lakes to enable pilots to get their bearings. In those early days of aviation, however, towns were difficult to identify from the air.

One Saturday as I hung around the airport I enviously watched Carl Gibson and a student practice take-offs and landings. After the lesson ended, Carl parked the plane and they climbed out. I listened as he talked with the student:

"You need to be thinking about flying cross-country before long. Keeping track of your position isn't easy. The towns look so much alike you can't tell 'em apart. What we need is a large sign with the name of the town on a prominent roof of each town and city. It would be a big help."

That gave me an idea. I asked Charlie Eggen whether the Chamber of Commerce would buy the paint if I volunteered to paint the name of the city on our hangar roof. He readily agreed, and I bought gallons of yellow paint. On Saturday, with yardstick, chalk and a long wooden straight edge, I laid out and painted GARDEN CITY in capital letters eight feet high.

"You did a great job," said Carl Gibson. "That'll make a lot of barnstormers happy!"

Charlie Eggen also was very pleased. "Marvin," he said, "if I write a letter introducing you to Chamber of Commerce officers around this area asking them to pay for the paint, would you like to go around to Deerfield, Lakin, Cimarron and other towns this summer and paint signs on the roofs?"

"Boy! I'd sure like to. I'll talk to my father and let you know."

Dad was all for it, but he did have one concern. "How're you going to get around to all those places?" he asked.

"I've got twenty-five dollars saved up. Charlie Weaver has an old Model T Ford for forty dollars, but it runs good. Could you lend me enough to buy it?"

The loan was arranged, and the Ford was loaded with paint brushes and equipment. Owning my own car was quite a thrill. I had learned to drive when I was 14 years old. A driver's license wasn't required in 1926. My father also had a Model T Ford, but I was only allowed to drive it on rare occasions.

I set off early on a summer morning with my carload of paint and a high heart. That summer I painted signs on roofs in eight western Kansas towns. I slept on the grass with a couple of blankets, and ate lots of peanut butter sandwiches.

Hank Winfield, a barnstorming pilot, put on an air show in Cimarron, Kansas, just as I completed a sign there. He was so pleased with the sign that he took me up for a free ride in his Travel Air cabin monoplane. He wanted to create some excitement, so he asked me to toss out a couple of live guinea hens for the crowd below.

We took off and climbed to 1,000 feet while I held a black and white speckled guinea hen in my arms, awaiting Hank's signal to release it. I could see the faces of the people on the ground, their hands shading their eyes as they watched us. Over the crowd by now, Hank gave me a thumbs up. I opened a window and threw the hens out, one after the other. We circled and watched as they fluttered to the ground, where dozens of people scrambled to catch them. Today there would be objections of cruelty to animals, but in those days we thought nothing of it.

Upon my graduation from high school in 1929, my family took a summer-long vacation to the west coast. Dad bought a new Model A Ford two-door sedan. It was a beautiful beige, which was truly remarkable considering that Henry Ford earlier had said, "People can have any color they want so long as it's black." Proud of our new car and in high spirits, Dad, Mom, my two younger brothers, Vernon and Herbert, and I headed west right after school let out.

A cross-country trip by automobile was a real adventure. We travelled on dirt roads for the most part. Highways were marked by painting a little mark on the telephone poles. If we had a flat tire we took the tire off, put rubber cement around the hole in the tube and placed a patch on it. We carried a tire pump to reinflate the tube. Burma Shave signs made the trip more interesting, the rhymed message being spread out over several signs along the roadside.

The trip was an aviation eye-opener for me. On the outskirts of Colorado Springs, Colorado, I spotted a row of airplanes. A sign read "Alexander Aircraft Company."

"Oh stop, Dad," I yelled, "I wanna look at those planes."

"Well, just for a few minutes." He obligingly pulled to the side of the road.

There was so much to see I didn't know where to start. The blue fuselage and silver wings of an Alexander Eaglerock three-passenger biplane glistened in the sunlight.

Except for a barbed wire fence surrounding the factory, there was no special security. I carefully wriggled through the fence and raced to the nearest plane. I loved the smell of fresh airplane "dope" (the liquid used to shrink the fabric covering the fuselage) filling the air. A mechanic in blue coveralls worked on an exposed engine.

"What kind of engine is that?" I asked.

"Curtiss OX5," he grunted, without pausing in his work.

I remembered reading about the OX5, but just to make sure, I asked, "Is it a 90 HP engine?"

"Yeah."

After World War I, thousands of surplus OX5 engines were sold to aircraft manufacturers for a pittance. Most of the airplanes built in the 1920's were powered with the OX5. They had radiators and were water-cooled. Air-cooled engines were just coming on the market. I stared in wonderment at the shiny new airplanes, as factory workers swarmed over them. I could willingly have spent several hours here but Dad honked the horn and yelled, "Come on...we gotta get going."

A few weeks later we arrived in Olympia, Washington after visiting Los Angeles. I spent three thrilling weeks in Olympia getting to know my pretty young cousin, Lorena Michael, a year younger than I. We stayed in her home with her parents and two brothers. Lorena and I hauled hay into the haymow, picked wild blackberries, hardly missed a day of swimming and had the time of our lives. Since I had no sisters, it was my first good opportunity to become well acquainted with a female.

Until now I had dated only two or three girls, and had not spent enough time with any of them to establish a close relationship. Lorena and I were together constantly. In the evenings we managed to get away from our families. We talked for hours on every conceivable subject. It was intoxicating! Eventually I summoned the courage to kiss her. She seemed to like it. Sadly, our close friendship had to come to an end, It was hard to say goodby.

We drove on to Spokane for another three weeks. While my family visited relatives, I took the streetcar each morning as far as it went toward Felts Field airport, and walked the rest of the way. A long row of hangars lined the south side of the field, parallel to the east-west runway. Fascinated with the sights, sounds and smells of a large airport, I put in long days familiarizing myself with all the different airplanes I'd been reading about.

One morning as I made my way down the line of hangars I joined two slightly younger boys. We slowly wandered around and eventually came to a huge Ford trimotor plane, affectionately known as the *Tin Goose.* Wow! I could hardly imagine how such a large plane could fly.

On the side of the plane, in large letters, I read, "Mamer Flying Service." Instead of the usual fabric, the plane was covered with corrugated aluminum alloy sheets—a bold step forward in airplane design. It was one of the first airplanes to have a cantilever wing. With strong internal bracing, the wing didn't need external wire or strut bracing. Just below the pilot's side window was the name "West Wind II." One engine was mounted in the nose. The other two hung beneath the high wing, one on either side of the fuselage. It carried a pilot, copilot, stewardess and eleven passengers.

As we walked admiringly around the plane, a slender man in his twenties wearing an airline uniform came out and asked, "Would you boys like to wash the plane for a ride in it?"

"Sure!" we enthusiastically replied as one.

"Come inside and I'll get you some stuff." In the hangar he gave us a broom, three pails of water, soap, and rags. He carried a stepladder out to the plane and said, "Wash off all the dirt real good—be sure the ladder doesn't bump against the plane. And for Pete's sake, don't climb on the tail!" He dipped a rag in water and showed us how to wash the plane, then left us to finish the job.

For a long and tiring three hours we worked feverishly, cleaning the big airplane inside and out. Art Walker, a rather short young man, came out and said, "Hey fellas, you did a great job! Climb in and we'll go for a ride." We scrambled up and sat in the wicker seats. The smell of new paint and leather was intoxicating. I felt very important riding where only rich people could ride. Mr. Walker was joined by the first man and they started the engines—one, two and three. We were all eyes and ears as the plane taxied to the end of the runway.

The pilots ran up each engine. Walker looked back and hollered, "Safety belts fastened?" We all nodded, and the giant plane rose into the air with a deafening roar. We were ecstatic, agog with the noise and vibration. With noses pressed to the windows, we studied the city below.

Meanwhile, the pilots moved switches and scrutinized instruments as they checked over the plane's performance. Satisfied everything was working well, they banked and turned toward the airport after a twenty-minute flight. We climbed out, all revved up. I asked Walker, "What's the other pilot's name?"

"Nick Mamer."

I thanked Walker again and rushed off to tell my parents of my big adventure. My ride in the Tin Goose was unquestionably the highlight of my summer of 1929. A few days after we left Spokane, Nick Mamer and Art Walker were in the headlines. They flew a Buhl Air Sedan for an endurance record by refueling in the air. I was in awe as I read about the Spokane Sun God, a biplane, being refueled with a hose lowered from another plane. They stayed in the air five days, travelling 7,200 miles across country and back. The scary part was when their propeller cut the refueling hose and they thought they'd be blown up from the explosion of the spilled fuel. But luck was with them and it didn't happen. As I read of their daring feat I could hardly wait to get my own airplane and set some world records!

High Schooler Marvin Michael looks over
Alexander Eaglerock. 1928

Chapter Two

HIGHER AND HIGHER

Garden City seemed very tame after our fantastic summer vacation. Now that my high school days were over, I needed to take the next step toward making my mark in the world of aviation. My parents couldn't afford to send me to college, and I had spent my meager savings on our trip. But with my dream still firmly in mind, at age seventeen I set my sights on the air capitol of the world. I packed my suitcase and hitchhiked to Wichita, Kansas, which in the late 1920's boasted no less than 25 airplane factories. I had taken two years of woodworking in high school. (We called it manual training.) I applied at several airplane factories for an apprentice job in their woodworking department. It was the only kind of job I thought I could handle. I went to Travel Air, Swallow and Cessna, without success.

At Stearman Aircraft I was interviewed by Clif Barron, their comptroller and office manager.

"I've had two years of woodworking in high school," I said hopefully, "and I'm looking for an apprentice job in your woodworking department."

Barron was a slight, sandy-haired man in his mid-thirties who spoke slowly and deliberately. In response to my earnest plea for a job he looked out of the window for a moment or two and finally, with a look of sympathy said, "I'm sorry, we don't have any woodworking jobs." I was crestfallen.

After a slight pause he asked, "Would you be interested in working as an office boy?" Fresh from small town and farm life, I had never even heard of an office boy.

"What would I be doing?" I asked.

"You'd open the incoming mail, sort and distribute it, fold, stuff, seal and stamp outgoing mail, escort visitors through the factory, and other miscellaneous jobs. Your starting salary would be $50 per month and we work 45 hours a week."

While in high school I had held summer farm jobs which paid $75 per month plus board and room, but farm jobs were backbreaking labor, and available only in the summer. I quickly accepted Barron's offer. I was so crazy about airplanes I would have worked for almost nothing. Thus began my aviation career.

One day Lloyd Stearman, president of Stearman Aircraft, handed me the keys to his Packard to take the company mail to the post office and said, "Don't crack it up." Boy! A 17-year-old kid driving a Packard! I enjoyed my moment of glory, and returned the car safely to its owner.

In the fall of 1930 I began my freshman year at McPherson College in Kansas. I was able to attend college with financial assistance from my brother, who was working as a printer's devil, for whom I later returned the favor. I transferred to Kansas State College as a sophomore in 1931. In addition to offering courses I needed, the good news about Kansas State was that it had a glider club, which I quickly joined. I looked forward eagerly to the time when I would actually get to fly. Unfortunately, the members first had to assemble the club's glider. We worked on it each Saturday of fall semester. Days and weeks dragged by and the autumn winds grew colder while we slowly put the glider together.

The Northrop primary glider was the minimum open framework contraption in which a man could fly. Dozens of brace wires held it together. There were no wheels on its landing gear—only a skid. When the final wire was in place there was cause for great celebration, and club members eagerly awaited a turn as pilot. To fly the machine, one sat strapped to a small square board below the leading edge of the wing, right hand on the control stick just ahead of the seat and feet resting on the rudder bar, which was connected by cables to the rudder.

The glider was launched with a rubber shock cord which operated like a slingshot. The midpoint of the cord was attached to the nose of the glider. Four men on each end of the cord stretched it forward in a V-shape while others held the tail. On a signal, the men released the tail and the glider shot off down the slope.

I watched with envy as other club members took their first flight. I critiqued their performance and made mental notes on how I would proceed when my turn arrived. On some Saturdays rain, wind, snow or glider repairs forced postponement of club activities. Each cancellation added to my impatience. Finally a beautiful clear day arrived, and wonder of wonders, it was time for my very first flight.

"Everybody ready?"

Then came the countdown. The launch team stretched the shock cord as I gripped the control stick in one hand and the glider seat in the other, bracing my head firmly against the back frame to prevent whiplash upon sudden acceleration.

"One, two, three, four, five—RUN!" On this command from their leader, the launch team members ran. On signal the glider tail was released, and I promptly was catapulted down the slope, feeling a tremendous sense of elation, They told me I was only about a foot above ground, but I flew! I really flew! It seemed to last only seconds.

After lunch I had another turn. This time the instructor advised: "We're going to send you up a little higher. Watch the rudder. Keep her going straight. Be careful not to stall, and try to keep your wings level."

How could I do all that in a few short seconds? I didn't have long to worry about it, because suddenly there was the countdown, and once more the thrill of shooting into the air. This time I was a lot higher—about twenty feet above ground. Glancing down, I panicked momentarily. What if the seat belt broke and I fell out? But it was exciting to get up so high. For fear of stalling I shoved the stick forward. Suddenly the ground came up fast. To avoid diving into it, I eased back on the stick. I touched the grass lightly, bounced into the air, and gently settled down. It was a smooth landing and the glider skidded easily to a halt.

The next year I transferred to Michigan to take aeronautical courses not available in Kansas. Compared to Kansas State, the University of Michigan Glider Club was like going from a Model T Ford to a Duesenberg. At the Ann Arbor airport we flew a Franklin secondary glider, a vast improvement over the Northrop primary.

The Franklin fuselage consisted of a fabric-covered welded-steel tubing framework, rather than an open framework. The pilot sat with only his head sticking out of the open cockpit. Below the pilot's seat a small rubber-tired wheel allowed the glider to accelerate quickly to flying speed and gently roll to a stop on landing. A skid on each wingtip prevented damage to the wing upon landing. We learned in easy stages by being towed along the runway behind a car at the end of a 150-foot wire. My instructor was Floyd Sweet, whose home town was Elmira, New York, considered the soaring capitol of the nation. Floyd was about 20-years-old and had been flying gliders for years. I admired his expertise.

"We start off towing you fast enough to keep the wings level and the glider going straight behind the tow car," said Floyd, "but not fast enough for you to get off the ground."

When we mastered those skills, we were towed a little faster so we could skim just above the ground. Later we were towed still faster, climbed to fifty feet, released the tow wire and experienced free flight.

Then Floyd said, "Now we're giving you a 900-foot wire. You should climb about 600 feet by the time the tow car slows down at the end of the runway and you release. Make a full circle flight back to the starting point. Don't try to land right at the beginning of the runway."

I followed his instructions to the T, and when I landed the glider after my 600 ft. circular flight, I had a tremendous feeling of accomplishment. This was really flying. Now I was indeed a pilot!

Having mastered the technique of soaring, my next challenge was to obtain pilot training, which was very expensive. I couldn't afford a commercial flight school and the obvious solution was to join the Army Air Corps (forerunner of the Air Force), which provided the finest flight training in the world.

After completing three years of college, during which my thoughts were constantly on flying, I meticulously filled out an application for military flight training. Then I waited. My excitement knew no bounds when in early 1934 the mail brought an appointment for my Air Force physical. By then I was back working at Stearman Aircraft, and took two days off to travel to Leavenworth, Kansas.

It was the most thorough physical exam I'd ever experienced, but I was confident throughout. The other young applicants and I went from one medical specialist to another. We were weighed, measured and tested for blood pressure, heart function, balance while blindfolded, and everything you could imagine.

After four hours of testing, the flight surgeon tried to be kind. "You got top marks in everything except eyesight," he said. "You have a slight astigmatism in your right eye. If you were already in the service you wouldn't be discharged. But your eyesight's not quite good enough to be accepted in the Air Corps. You should be wearing glasses."

My stomach knotted. I was devastated. I couldn't believe it. Surely the doctor had made a terrible mistake. In desperation I asked, "What about the Navy—could I pass their test?"

"No, their requirements are identical to ours."

"What if I took eye exercises?"

"They wouldn't correct astigmatism."

"Could I get contact lenses?"

"The doctor would detect them immediately, and they're not permitted."

I sat in stunned silence. Sensing my frustration, the doctor consoled me.

"I know it's a great disappointment to you. You've done so well in all the other tests. I'm sure you'll succeed in something else to your liking."

It was small consolation. He extended his hand and smiled. I thanked him and slowly headed for the door.

Crawling into bed that night, I couldn't hold back the tears. I had been so sure I would pass. Failing the physical exam had been the farthest thing from my mind. At work my thoughts kept returning to my flunkout. I'd always been blessed with boundless optimism, but now it was gone. I was in deep depression. Night after night I lay awake wondering why this had happened and considering what, if anything, I could do about it.

Gradually the gloom lifted as alternatives began to come to mind. Failing the Air Corps exam did not mean I had to give up my dream of flying. After all, the eye doctor had said I would be able to fly an airplane if I wore glasses. I felt fortunate that I would be able to continue flying gliders when I returned to the University from my Stearman job. Flying gliders would be an important step toward my goal of becoming a professional pilot.

Meanwhile my desire to fly an airplane remained uppermost in my mind. I asked Monty Barnes, a wheeler-dealer FBO (Fixed Base Operator) if he knew of a low-priced used airplane I could buy. He told me of a Waco 9 biplane, minus engine, that was for sale "as is" for $100. It had been dismantled and stored in a barn, but Monty said he could haul it to Wichita for me.

"Don't worry about the engine," Monty told me. "I'll sell you one—make you a good price."

What he didn't tell me was that he had enough Curtiss OX5 engine parts in his garage to assemble an engine.

"I'll show you how to put it together," he said.

I was able to rent hangar space for very little in the Beech factory, which had been shut down by the Great Depression. By November the unheated hangar was bitter cold, however, and my fingers wouldn't work very well. Monty Barnes' assurances of help in putting the plane and engine together didn't amount to much, because just when I needed his instructions, he was always off on a charter flight.

Finally in February 1934, the airplane was assembled and rigged, and the engine was hung.

John Roby, a skilled OX5 mechanic, and I pushed the plane outside the hangar to check out the engine. We chocked the wheels and I climbed in the cockpit.

Roby stood by the propeller and called, "Switch off."

I responded, "Switch off."

He pulled the propeller through four revolutions and called, "Contact."

I called back, "Contact."

He raised his left leg, brought it down, and gave a powerful yank on the propeller. To my surprise, the engine sprang to life.

"Whoopee!" I yelled.

I warmed up the engine, then gradually gave it full throttle. The powerful roar was music to my ears. The exhaust had an aroma of its own—no car exhaust ever quickened my pulse like this! I slowly closed the throttle and turned off the ignition. We pushed the plane back into the hangar to do some final rigging on the flying and landing wires.

Several weeks went by. I was too busy to go out to complete the job, and suddenly it was time for me to go back to the University to continue my studies. I was keenly disappointed at not getting to fly the plane at least once. With deep regret, I sold it to Monty Barnes for just a few dollars more than I had paid for its unassembled parts. I needed the money for school expenses.

* * * *

Back in school once more, the winter months crept slowly by. I grew restless sitting in classes dealing with lift, drag and horsepower. At last the snows melted and crocuses burst into bloom. Cloudy skies gave way to sunny days.

R.E. Franklin, mechanical engineering professor and designer of the Franklin glider, suggested a soaring expedition to Sleeping Bear Sand Dune in northern Michigan. It was a legendary gathering place of the Indians, and more recently famous as the world's largest sand dune, which was fast becoming a mecca for midwest soaring enthusiasts. The world offered only two favorably developed soaring locales—the Wasserkuppe in Germany and Harris Hill at Elmira, New York. Members of our glider club jumped at R.E.'s suggestion.

"We tow along the Lake Michigan beach," he said. "We can easily get 800 feet of altitude on the tow."

In June 1936 I took off from the shore of Lake Michigan and soared over Sleeping Bear Sand Dune, which rises steeply for 700 feet above the lake. The winds from the lake blew against the ridge and were deflected upward. In this rising air current, I flew back and forth above and in front of the ridge. After five minutes in the air it started raining. Not to be defeated by the elements, I flew more slowly to keep the rain from stinging my face and hung on through fifteen minutes of downpour.

Three other fellows were waiting to fly, so after 39 minutes I knew I should land on the narrow beach. One wing tip nearly brushed the side of the bluff, and the other projected out over Lake Michigan, thus requiring a precision landing. With a slight deviation to the left the wing tip would strike the ridge. A deviation to the right would have sink the glider in the lake. That flight earned my "C" soaring badge, authenticated by the French organization, the Federation Aeronautique Internationale.

R.E. was a superb cook, and had brought complete camping gear. We inhaled the aroma of the delicious meal he prepared on his Coleman stove, and stew never tasted so good. After dinner we sat around in the lantern light, reliving the events of the day.

"I never dreamed soaring could be so much fun," I said. "You just sit there, flying effortlessly back and forth along the ridge."

"You need to be thinking about flying in the National Soaring Contest in Elmira, New York," R.E. told us. "You'll be doing thermal soaring as well as ridge soaring there."

"How does thermal soaring work?" I asked him.

"The sun heats the ground, the ground heats the air above it, and bubbles of hot air rise up. When you fly into one of these thermals, you start circling, and it takes you up, 'til the lift peters out, or you lose it."

Days later, we packed our glider on the trailer and headed for Elmira.

I felt some trepidation as I awaited my first flight at Elmira, in the June 1936 Seventh Annual National Soaring Contest. Four fellows held the tail while a car stretched the rubber shock cord attached to the nose of the glider.

"All set?"

I nodded, and when the cord had the proper amount of stretch the tow-car driver dropped his red flag. I shouted "Let go!" and the fellows released the tail. Immediately I was catapulted at terrific speed over the car and shot off the top of East Hill. Fear gripped me as I reached 1500 feet above the valley floor. The panic quickly subsided and I soared back and forth along the ridge, dodging eight other gliders. Watching them closely helped me determine where the upward air currents were the strongest. Whenever a glider rose rapidly, I headed in that direction in an effort to get some of his lift. With so many gliders hugging the ridge, mid-air collisions might seem likely. However, visibility from a glider is excellent—better than from an airplane. We seldom had to alter course, because we could readily see that we could pass the other glider above, below, or to one side. After 45 minutes I landed in a clover field in the valley below.

Next day I took off from Harris Hill soaring head-quarters and climbed to 2100 feet above the valley. This was the most enjoyable flight of all. From this elevation, I could see mountains in the distance. There is usually good lift below a billowing cumulus cloud. I tried several times to catch onto a cloud, which might enable me to fly 10 or 15 miles cross-country, but couldn't get high enough. After an hour and nine minutes I landed back on Harris Hill, having earned the tidy sum of $15.66 prize money.

But now it was time to leave this heady atmosphere and come down to earth. I needed to get back to my Stearman job in Wichita, a thousand miles to the west, but first I had a pilgrimage to make. My usual mode of transportation was readily available; I headed for the nearest highway and raised my thumb.

Marvin Michael in University of Michigan Glider Club's Franklin secondary glider. 1932-1938

Chapter Three

FROM PLANE TO TRAIN

I was a senior at the University of Michigan in 1935, and worked for my room rent in The Baptist Guild House, a 60-year old, three-story brick building owned by the Ann Arbor First Baptist Church, which was across the street. The first floor was devoted to student activities sponsored by the church. Doctor and Mrs. Chapman (he was pastor to the university students) lived on the second floor, and my roommate and I lived on the third floor. The Chapmans were an elderly couple. Frail Mrs. Chapman was from New England, and was very proper. As Christmas break approached she spoke to me one day while I was vacuuming carpets. "Marvin, what are your plans for the holidays?"

"I've signed up to drive a new car from the factory in Detroit to Washington state, for free transportation. I'll visit my parents in Olympia. I'm feeling a little homesick...I haven't been home for three years."

Mrs. Chapman thought that sounded like a great opportunity for me to spend Christmas with my family. "Be sure to tell me all about it when you return," she said.

Hitchhiking the 35 miles to Detroit was no big deal; students did it all the time. I learned I'd be driving one of six new Essex Terraplanes from the auto factory to Aberdeen, Washington.

The Essex Terraplane was a lower priced car built by the Hudson Motor Company. Mr. Koppenhofer, the Hudson dealer from Aberdeen was a big blond German fellow.

"We're going to hook two cars together with a special towbar," he explained. "That way, we only need three drivers instead of six. We'll each tow a car."

The car deliveries from the factory were three days late. I stayed in a cheap hotel and existed mostly on hamburgers until we received the cars. Hooking them up with towbars further postponed our departure. My precious vacation time was melting away as these unforeseen delays ate away at the time I would be able to spend with my parents. Four days ticked past, and I was feeling very frustrated. Maybe this wasn't such a good idea after all, but I couldn't back out now.

At last we were ready to go. What a thrill to drive a brand new car! The shiny brown body sparkled in the winter sunlight. The quiet engine purred smoothly, and there was that great new car smell. We drove the tandem cars in a caravan. There wasn't much traffic on the highway, especially at Christmas time.

All went well until we hit icy highways in Iowa. Because of the added drag of the towed car, we had to gain a dangerously high speed while descending one hill in order to make it up the next. My palms were sweating as I tried to judge how fast I could safely go downhill. It was a nightmare. The other two drivers were facing the same problem. When we reached Des Moines the dealer decided to disconnect the cars and look for three additional drivers, causing yet another additional delay. At that point, however, he agreed to let me go on ahead.

The next day was Christmas. Driving at moderate speed on hard-packed snow in Nebraska, I honked to warn a bicyclist that I would be passing him. At the very last moment, and without warning he swerved to the left in front of me. With a quick reflex action I turned the car to the left, whereupon it rolled completely over in the ditch, stopping right side up. I got out of the car and was surprised to see that two boys had been riding a brand new Christmas bicycle. They were about twelve years old, frightened and crying, standing by their slightly bent red bicycle.

"Didn't you hear me honk?" I asked. They were wearing caps covering their ears.

"Naw. We can't hear much with these caps."

Without my quick reaction I'd have killed them both! I was greatly relieved to find that they were only bruised and scratched. There was no mark on the front of my car, but red bicycle paint on the right rear fender indicated that they had run into me, and not vice versa.

A tow truck pulled me out, we straightened a couple of fenders, and the car drove OK. Way behind schedule by now, I hurried on, arriving in Olympia about midnight two days later. At my parents' house I knocked three times, before the folks woke up. Dad sleepily opened the door and then hollered, "Elsie, Marvin's here!" He gave me a big hug. "We're sure glad to see you. We were getting worried."

I briefly explained what had happened, concluding with, "I'm exhausted. I drove 820 miles, stopping only to eat. Let's hit the hay and I'll fill you in tomorrow." After breakfast next morning Dad drove with me to Aberdeen and I delivered the car to the dealer.

"What the hell happened?" Mr. Koppenhofer exploded, and followed up with a string of profanity. "I didn't have any insurance on these cars. You've left me in a helluva mess!"

I explained that I had to roll the car to avoid killing two boys. "It was a totally unavoidable accident," I said. "Here are the names and addresses of the boys' parents so you can collect damages from them."

"There's no way I can sue them way back in Nebraska!"

"I'm terribly sorry, Mr. Koppenhofer—it couldn't be helped." I felt bad for him, but as I saw it, I had an unavoidable accident which wasn't my fault. Dad and I left while the unhappy car dealer was still fuming.

As my brief one-day visit with Dad and Mom was about to end, Dad asked, "How are you going to get back to Ann Arbor?"

"I'm going to hitchhike," I said.

Dad pulled out his wallet. "Here's fifteen dollars for bus fare. We'll drive you to Portland where you can catch a more direct bus." About 4 p.m. they dropped me off at a service station in Portland. Even though I knew that fifteen dollars bus fare would take me from Olympia to Ann Arbor, I had other thoughts. I was obsessed with the desire to know and experience everything about airplanes.

In my aeronautical engineering course I was getting into the study of airlines. I'd been reading about the highly advanced new Boeing 247 passenger plane.

As soon as my parents were out of sight, I ran into the service station and phoned United Airlines.

"When does your next eastbound plane leave?"

"Six o'clock."

"How far can I go for fifteen dollars?"

"We can take you to Pendleton, Oregon, for twelve dollars and thirty cents."

"I'd like to make a reservation. I'll pay for my ticket at the airport in about half an hour."

I hitchhiked to Swan Island airport. The agent who sold me my ticket asked, "Where are you heading for?"

"Ann Arbor, Michigan. I'm a student at the University of Michigan."

"How are you going to get from Pendleton to Ann Arbor?"

"I'm gonna hitchhike."

Smelling a story for airline publicity, he phoned a newspaper. They promptly sent a reporter who asked more questions.

"Why are you spending your bus money for a short airplane ride?"

"Because I've never flown on an airline, or flown at night. I want to see what it's like. It'll help me in my airplane design classes."

By now I was so excited I could hardly wait. For an interminable hour I sat down, got up, paced around the terminal, and sat down again. Finally, shortly after dark, another man and I boarded a Boeing Model 247 ten-passenger twin-engined plane. This innovative airplane was the first all-metal transport, and it revolutionized airplane design. The retractible landing gear was a brand new feature. The fuselage was mounted atop the wing so that the landing gear could retract into the full cantilever wing. The spar from wingtip to wingtip was similar to a bridge truss. By definition, cantilever wings have no external strut or wire bracing, so the spar which provided the strength in bending had to be very wide and deep. It took up so much space in the cabin floor that when walking from the cabin to the cockpit one had to step over the 18-inch high spar.

What a thrill to feel the powerful acceleration on takeoff and to see the millions of lights in the city below! I hadn't dreamed a city would have so many lights, or that the lights would outline the streets so clearly. What luxury, I thought, to be sitting in this plush seat where usually only wealthy people sit! I was entranced by the smell of new leather and the powerful roar of the engines.

Up to this time I'd had only three or four brief rides with barnstormers in old biplanes. What a difference! I imagined I was the captain in the lefthand seat. Through my window I searched the ground for anything recognizable. Except for a few small towns we flew over, it was pitch black. Twice we passed rotating beacons— powerful searchlights to aid the pilot in navigation. When there were no more lights on the ground, I guessed we were over the mountains. I was fascinated and exhilarated!

Twenty minutes into the flight, the stewardess served us an apple and a doughnut. Seeing eight empty seats, I asked her, "Why can't I just stay on the plane beyond Pendleton?"

She said, "I'm sorry—it's strictly against the rules."

"May I ask the captain?"

"Yes you can, but I'm sure that's what he'll say."

An hour after takeoff the stewardess told us we'd be landing in Pendleton in a few minutes. Even with the best of luck, it would have taken about eight hours to hitchhike.

Before we landed the stewardess gave me a sack with three apples and three doughnuts, a most welcome gift! I'm sure she felt sorry for me, knowing that I would be hitchhiking in the freezing weather. Upon landing I waited for the captain to come down the steps. Slender, in his snappy uniform and carrying his flight case, he couldn't have been more than thirty-five. I was afraid he'd say no but I had to ask.

"Sir, since there are so many empty seats, couldn't I just stay on the plane? It wouldn't cost United anything!"

"I'd like to," he replied, "but I couldn't possibly do it. I'd lose my job." I felt he really meant it.

With a sense of despair, I watched the plane take off and climb into the night sky, carrying four people and nine empty seats.

Hitchhiking along the snow-covered highways of eastern Oregon and Idaho in the middle of a northern winter was a fiasco. The Great Depression had severely curtailed all kinds of travel. By this time I had hitchhiked more than 20,000 miles to and from college, but it was excruciating standing in a near zero biting wind, sticking out my thumb at the few passing cars.

After obtaining rides for only 300 miles in two freezing days I realized that at this rate I'd never make my Monday morning class. It was crucial that I be there because this was my toughest subject and I was struggling to keep up. In desperation I decided to hop a freight train.

During the Depression thousands of men and a few women rode freight trains, mostly in search of jobs. I had learned the technique of boarding trains by reading *Boy and Girl Tramps of America* by John Compton. I knew the railroad "bulls" would chase me away if they caught me loitering in the freight yard. I had to keep out of sight until the engineer gave two short blasts on the whistle and the train started moving. Then I would have to run like mad and jump on. I realize in retrospect that I was very foolish to have risked life and limb in this manner. Many have fallen under the wheels, severed a leg and bled to death in the attempt.

Several freight trains brought me to Grand Rapids, Michigan by Sunday evening, but I was frustrated to learn that there would not be a freight train to get me to Ann Arbor in time for my Monday morning class. My only chance was a passenger train. During the Depression the railroads generally tolerated riding freights. Hopping passenger trains, however, was a serious misdemeanor, calling for 30 days in jail.

I waited out of sight in the darkness until the engineer blew his whistle. As the train slowly accelerated, I ran and climbed up onto the front end of the forward baggage car, just behind the tender. I sat crossways in the telescoping blind that would connect it to another car ahead. The clickety-clack of the wheels was music to my ears.

Just as I was congratulating myself that I would make that eight o'clock class after all, I suddenly was deluged with what seemed like tons of icy water. I panicked! I felt the blood draining from my face. My heart beat wildly. What I didn't know was that this locomotive took water on the fly to save time. While in motion, a scoop was extended down into a trough of water. Most of the water went into the tender, but copious amounts spilled out. Fortunately the temperature was below freezing, so the water froze on my heavy overcoat instead of soaking through.

When the train stopped in Ann Arbor I jumped off and hiked up the hill to my room. I was covered with soot and icicles and I didn't want Mrs. Chapman to see me in this condition. I opened the front door very cautiously, but it squeaked loudly. Mrs. Chapman, on the second floor stair landing asked, "Who's there?"

"It's Marvin," I tried to speak nonchalantly.

"Oh Marvin, how was your trip?"

I was stuck! I climbed the stairs and stood before her on the dimly lit landing. "Overall it was a wonderful trip," I replied, "But the car I drove was delivered three days late and we lost another day in Iowa because the roads were icy. Because of all the delays I only had one day to visit my folks but it was great to see them. Dad gave me the money for my first airline flight— from Portland to Pendleton, Oregon. I hitchhiked the rest of the way."

"My, that was quite an experience! We'll have to hear more about it tomorrow." If Mrs. Chapman was able to perceive my miserable appearance in the dim light, she was too nice to comment on it.

I made my eight o'clock class on time!

Beloved "Putt Putter," a 36 horsepower Aeronca C-3 two seater. It landed in nearly every cow pasture and wheat field in Kansas. 1936

Chapter Four

HOLD THE PRESSES!

On graduating from the University of Michigan in 1936 I returned to my former employer in Wichita. Back at the Stearman Aircraft Company I enjoyed my work as a stress analyst and aerodynamicist. While I had been away at college, the great test pilot, Eddie Allen, spent some time at Stearman conducting flight tests on their Northrop plane. Everyone at Stearman thought he was charming and they were so full of praise for this freelance test pilot that I determined I would meet him at the first opportunity.

I had a great feeling of accomplishment now that I had that sheepskin and a good job which utilized the skills I had worked hard at learning. But there was a part of my dream that still occupied my thoughts much of the time. Not even the Great Depression could dampen my desire to fly.

On a bright summer day shortly after I was back at Stearman, I walked into the Hart Flying Service at the Wichita airport, which was a square mile of prairie sod with no paved runways. Things seemed quiet at the flying service. The only person in sight was a slender young fellow in his twenties, who sat on a sofa, reading an aviation magazine. He was the person in charge and also the flying instructor. Looking up he asked, "What can I do for you?"

"How much do you charge for dual time?" I asked.

"$4.50 an hour."

"I've flown gliders quite a bit...more than forty hours," I said. "I'm interested in taking some dual time in a plane to see how valuable my gliding experience will be in flying an airplane."

"OK. Sounds like you've pretty well mastered air work—we'll shoot some takeoffs and landings."

The obliging young man, whose name was Wade Johnson, and I climbed into the two-passenger Taylor Cub high-wing monoplane. (Piper later bought out Taylor, giving rise to the famous Piper Cub.) Johnson sat in the front seat and I sat in the rear. Turning around to face me, he said, "When we reach 500 feet altitude, throttle back to 2200 RPM, make a shallow left turn and head north."

A mechanic swung the propeller to start the little four-cylinder, 40 horsepower Continental engine. The first surprise came when Johnson turned around again. "OK, taxi it straight out west a ways, and then we'll take off to the south." I had thought he would at least taxi the ship out and make the first takeoff! I was nervous but thrilled that I was to have that honor.

After I taxied the plane out and made the south turn, Johnson took a final look around for other planes, then told me to gently ease the throttle forward all the way and make the takeoff. What if somehow I lost control and damaged the plane? But to my surprise the takeoff was fairly smooth. It felt almost like flying a glider.

At 500 feet altitude I throttled back, turned left and headed north as instructed. What a thrill to be actually flying an airplane! Looking down at the ground on the left, where we'd be landing, I tried to decide when to start my next turn. At the north end of the airport, I throttled back and turned left. With the throttle closed, airplanes descend more steeply than gliders, so my glider experience led me to cut the throttle too soon. My heart skipped a beat when I saw we were headed right for some telephone wires. I opened the throttle a bit, and we cleared them nicely.

I was confident of my flying ability, yet this was quite different from a glider. Would I botch the landing, the most dangerous part of the flight? About 50 feet above the ground I started easing back on the stick, just as I had done many times in gliders. We landed with the tail not quite down in the three-point position. Tail-high landings in gliders are proper, but in airplanes the tail should touch at the same time as the wheels.

The plane made a slight bounce into the air, and instinctively I shoved the stick forward rapidly to correct. Johnson quickly took control, pulled the stick back, gunning the engine at the same time. After we stopped, he explained, "Planes are different from gliders. You should gun the engine and keep the stick back. If you over-react in pushing the stick forward, you could nose over and land upside down!"

We made several more landings, each one a little better, but still rough. After the sixth landing, Johnson climbed out of the ship. Did I land so hard he has to inspect the landing gear, I wondered.

Instead he said, "I'm gonna let you take it by yourself this time."

I couldn't believe it. This was terrific! There hadn't even been one smooth landing yet. Did he think I was good enough to solo already? But I didn't question him— I *knew* I could do it. My excitement mounted at the thought of my long-dreamed-of first solo!

"You don't have very much gas," Johnson warned, "so only make one flight around the pattern and taxi back in."

As I opened the throttle and started roaring across the grass with an empty seat in front of me, my total concentration was on completing a safe solo flight. The plane climbed more quickly with only one person aboard. I made my turn and headed back for the north end of the field. Forward visibility was better with the instructor gone and it helped. I made a perfect landing on my first solo. After many years of waiting and wishing, I had successfully flown an airplane on my own! It's hard to describe the feeling of exhilaration that came over me as I climbed out of the plane and received Wade Johnson's warm congratulations.

The next day at work I became something of a hero when fellow workers produced a clipping from the morning paper. It was a story describing me as a young Stearman Aircraft Company engineer who soloed an airplane after 35 minutes' instruction, when 12 hours is usual.

Now that I had soloed it made a lot of sense to me that I should have my own airplane, and the fact that I was a rather impecunious recent college graduate on his first full-fledged job didn't deter me. At a time when other young fellows of similar circumstance were visiting used-car lots and kicking tires of possible vehicles, I was making the rounds to study available airplanes.

From my somewhat unorthodox viewpoint an automobile was not a necessity, but an airplane was.

A few months later I bought a used airplane affectionately known as the bathtub Aeronca, because its nose was shaped like the back of an old-fashioned bathtub. Two people sat side-by-side in it. Instead of the more usual smooth staccato engine sound, my diminutive 36 HP, two-cylinder Aeronca seemed to say "putt-putt-putt-putt." The little plane became my beloved "Putt-putter."

Of my $135 monthly salary, I paid an $80 airplane payment, $10 hangar rent and $10 for gas and oil. That left $35 a month for lodging, meals and clothing. By renting light housekeeping rooms which I shared with four young men and cooking my own meals, I managed to get by.

Putt-putter was my life. One of my roommates, Dutch Rawdon, was a pilot and gave me a few flying lessons. Dutch was a genial fellow, younger than I. He had a tendency to shirk some of his household duties, but he was so lovable we let him get by with it. Soon I became brave enough to venture off cross-country, using a road map for navigation. Putt-putter and I landed in scores of cow pastures and wheat fields all over Kansas.

Some of the planes being made were difficult to recover from a tailspin. Many pilots died when their planes spun into the ground. The Civil Aviation Administration (later named the Federal Aeronautics Authority) therefore, required applicants to demonstrate precision recovery from a spin in order to earn a pilot's license.

Dutch showed me how to enter a tailspin by pulling the stick back hard. I learned that just before the plane stalled, I must kick full rudder. The nose then dropped, pointing nearly straight down, and the plane went round and round. It was scary.

I was apprehensive the first time I practiced spins without Dutch's presence to keep me out of trouble. After climbing to about 3,000 feet, Putt-putter spun straight down, and the ground seemed so close I panicked. My stomach felt like it would jump out of my mouth. I was sure I could never recover before crashing. What if I had forgotten my spin recovery technique or it didn't work this time? Before I could wet my pants, Putt-putter recovered and I was flying straight and level. What a relief! As I continued to practice spins, each one bolstered my confidence. I rehearsed tailspins and all sorts of precision maneuvers in preparation for the flight check for my private pilot license.

By the time I took my flight check with a CAA inspector I felt fairly confident, but nervous. Pilots call it inspectoritis. Still, the maneuvers went OK with the inspector at my side. "You did a good job," he said at the end of the test. My joy was ecstatic when I finally received that coveted license. Now I could take passengers in Putt-putter. And I did carry lots of them, with a great sense of satisfaction.

Thanks to Putt-putter, that first year after college was one of my happiest times. I worked hard on my job, but my real joy came whenever I was able to slide into the cockpit, perhaps with a friend along, and explore by air the Kansas countryside. I continued to give thought to my future, however, and realized that I should aspire to an advanced degree. Eight months into my year at Stearman this avenue suddenly was opened to me.

The telegram read, "COMMITTEE HAS AWARDED YOU $600 SHEEHAN SCHOLARSHIP FOR 1937-38 ACADEMIC YEAR. WIRE IMMEDI-

ATELY IF YOU CAN ACCEPT," signed UNIVERSITY OF MICHIGAN SCHOLARSHIP COMMITTEE.

I cheered 'til I was hoarse! Of course I would accept, but what would I study in graduate school? Despite my inability to enter the Army Air Corps, I had not given up the hope of becoming a professional pilot. But I was in a quandary as to what studies I should pursue at this point. I felt the need of a mentor who could advise me, and although I had not yet managed to meet him, the great test pilot Eddie Allen came immediately to mind. I so admired him and wanted to follow in his footsteps. I thought if I wrote to him he might offer some suggestions on what I should study in order to combine an aeronautical engineering and flying job. But I worried that he'd be too important a man, too busy to reply to a young fellow he had never met. I decided to give it a try anyway. Even a one-paragraph reply dictated to his secretary could be helpful.

Sooner than I expected and to my great delight, back came a three-page hand-written letter. I shall never forget nor shall I ever lose the inspiration of his opening sentence:

"Your letter interested me very much because it well expresses the grand struggle against big odds toward an achievement." He continued: *"Get a job as a flight test engineer with a large company, since the small companies don't have the resources to do flight test research. Study aerodynamics; that will give you the best background for flight test engineering. It will provide the greatest possibility of a career combining engineering with flying."*

That settled it. I returned to the University of Michigan to obtain my master's degree in aerodynamics. His letter determined my career, and his inspiration was to play a major role in my life. I looked forward to meeting him some day.

World famous test pilot Eddie Allen and Boeing
Model 314 Clipper. 1940

Chapter Five

COME FLY WITH ME

I returned in the fall of 1937 to the University of
Michigan. It seemed good to be back on campus except
for one thing; I had to leave my little bathtub Aeronca
behind. Since scholarships were only for poor boys in
those days, I didn't think it would look right to take
beloved Putt-putter to Ann Arbor. Reluctantly I stored
her in a barn, promising that we wouldn't be parted for
long. This was a painful sacrifice, particularly since two
other students brought their own airplanes to Ann Arbor. Obviously their parents were better off than mine,
and they were not scholarship students.

Upon graduation in June, Stearman asked me to stay
in Ann Arbor for summer session, hire some students,
and supervise tests of their Model X-100 twin engine
light attack bomber in the University wind tunnel.

One fateful summer evening I went to the Graduate School get-acquainted party at the Women's League
ballroom. There I met a beautiful young coed. Her voice

was soft and smooth and her large brown eyes had a twinkle that captivated me. Her charming smile turned me on with a bang.

"I'm Marvin Michael—what's your name?"

"Laura Moser."

"Where are you from, Laura?"

"Pennsylvania."

"Whereabouts in Pennsylvania?"

"Indiana."

"Wait a minute. I thought you said Pennsylvania."

"Indiana, Pennsylvania. Indiana's the name of the city."

Laura was a high school literature teacher, and obviously was intelligent in addition to being very pretty, a combination which appealed greatly to me. We found we had a similar background. My father was the pastor of several churches, and her father had been superintendent of Sunday schools in Pennsylvania for the Lutheran Church.

On our second date I asked, "How'd you like to go for an airplane ride on our next date?"

"Sounds great. Are you a pilot?"

"Yes."

We went to the Ann Arbor airport where I had made hundreds of glider flights and as a graduate student had rented small planes as often as my budget would allow. We walked over to a shiny yellow Aeronca K, a later model than Putt-putter. It was more streamlined and flew faster.

I helped Laura into the passenger seat and fastened her seat belt, then slid into the left seat. The waiting mechanic made a swift pull on the prop and the engine leaped to life. I taxied the plane out to the end of the runway and took off.

We flew over Ann Arbor, then circled the University campus. "Can you pick out your dormitory?" I yelled above the clatter of the engine. She nodded. What a thrill to know that she trusted me enough to fly with me! Although I enjoyed an occasional steep turn or wingover, I didn't want to scare her so I flew straight and level and made gentle turns.

"How do you like it?" I shouted.

"It's wonderful!" she said enthusiastically. I was on an emotional high, introducing the girl who already had become very special to me to flying, the abiding love of my life. I'm afraid I'd have lost interest in her if she hadn't shown some excitement.

During our whirlwind courtship we played a lot of early morning tennis. In the evenings we sat on the steps in the lighted entrance of a classroom building. She read me Kahlil Gibran's *The Prophet* and many poems. It was bliss! Obviously she was a superior teacher of literature, and I thought her students were very fortunate. By now I was thoroughly under Laura's spell. I found a handkerchief she had dropped. For days I'd close my eyes, take a whiff of her perfume, and revel in the thought of her beauty. We fell in love and became engaged, with plans to be married the following spring.

My wind tunnel tests and summer school ended at almost the same time. Laura returned to Pennsylvania to fulfill her teaching contract and I went back to my job at Stearman. The remaining months of 1938 stretched dismally ahead for me because Laura and I were so many miles apart. It didn't seem like there was anything that could cheer me up, but I was in for a wonderful surprise.

My supervisor at Stearman called me in one day to tell me that Eddie Allen would be arriving to conduct test flights on Stearman's Model X-100 light attack bomber, and I was to serve as his flight engineer!

It seemed a miraculous turn of events that because of the letter I had written Allen two years earlier and his inspiring reply, I had obtained the additional education which now qualified me to assist him on his test flights.

One morning shortly thereafter I was out in the Stearman final assembly sticking yarn tufts on the Model X-100 in preparation for stall tests when I saw a stranger approaching the plane as if he were studying every detail of its design. He was accompanied by several Stearman executives, and suddenly I realized that I was at last going to meet my mentor, Eddie Allen, face to face. He was in his early forties, small of stature, had a receding hairline, and probably weighed about 140 lbs. I later saw him described as "frail as a wisp of smoke" and I agreed.

As he drew near I turned to him saying, "I'm Marvin Michael. I wrote you..." He flashed a warm smile of recognition as he said, "Oh, Marvin Michael! Yes, sure, I remember the letter you wrote." I was greatly in awe of this man, but his warm friendliness helped me to relax in his presence. I watched him inspect the X-100, impressed with his methodical and thorough manner.

Several days later he asked, "Marvin, would you like to come up to my room at the Allis Hotel tonight? Maybe we can visit and discuss airplanes." I was elated, yet I went with trepidation. I had never been this close to anyone as famous as Eddie. Although I was fresh out of graduate school, I hadn't yet had time to apply my newfound knowledge on the job. Would I be able to talk intelligently and comfortably with such a genius?

He quickly put me at ease. "You wrote that you recently got your private pilot license," he said. "Tell me about it." We reminisced about my letter and his reply. He seemed genuinely interested in what I'd learned in graduate studies. We talked about boundary layer control, the technique of channeling airflow around a wing to make an airplane land more slowly. I mentioned a recent boundary layer article I'd read in the *Journal of Aeronautical Sciences*. He hadn't seen the article, and asked me to tell him about it. As I said goodby and walked out the door, my feet never touched the floor.

"It seems really terrific that a young fellow like me can tell Eddie Allen something new," I thought proudly.

Too quickly his part of the testing was completed and he returned to the Boeing Company in Seattle, while I felt very fortunate to be paid for doing what I enjoyed the most—flying as a flight test engineer.

I of course had a lot to tell Laura about the thrill of working with someone as respected and skilled as Eddie Allen. Letters and phone calls helped to strengthen our bond as we made plans for our wedding.

"Sweetheart," I said, "I've got a great idea. For our honeymoon let's fly Putt-putter to Colorado Springs. We can enjoy lots of wonderful sightseeing there. It's a perfect place to honeymoon."

"Oh, no!" she said. "Colorado Springs is OK, but I don't want to fly in that little plane."

"Why not?"

"I just don't." I was extremely disappointed, but I realized I couldn't win this one.

In the spring of 1939 Laura flew to Wichita, and it was wonderful to see her again. We borrowed my parents' car for our honeymoon. I realized that it really didn't matter what form of transportation we chose; the important thing was being together. After a simple morning wedding, we drove to another city. On checking into the hotel that evening, the desk clerk said to the bellhop, "Take them to the bridal suite." How did he know we were just married?

Fortunately Laura's objections to a flying honeymoon didn't foreshadow a real antipathy to Putt-putter. During the early years of our marriage we had many a skyborne adventure as she shared my interest in casting our little airplane's shadow over as many square miles of Kansas as possible. It was a new way of life for her, and she showed herself to be a really good sport about some of our hairier adventures. She wrote about one of these to friends back in Pennsylvania.

Wings! What magic lay in their span. As the new bride of a pilot-engineer, I too wanted to discover that enchantment. We were preparing to take my first flight in Putt-putter, Marvin's little Aeronca two-seater.

"How are we going to get to the airport?" I asked Marvin.

"Take a bus to the city limits and hitchhike the rest of the way," was his matter-of-fact reply.

"Hitchhike?" I gasped incredulously. But I had heard correctly. An airplane and a car together were beyond our budget as newlyweds, so Marvin's dearly beloved Putt-putter stayed with us while the car had to wait.

Hitchhiking was better than expected, however. Marvin seemed quite skilled at the process (after 25,000 miles of experience) and soon obtained the necessary ride for us. Before long we were squeezing ourselves into our diminutive flying carpet, boasting all of 36 hp.

Another thirty minutes found us miles from Wichita, having a hilarious time skimming the treetops at 60 miles per hour, looking down in sheer delight at the farmhouses

200 feet below. We never ceased laughing at the spectacle of dozens of tiny white dots which we knew were horror-stricken chickens flapping their wings wildly in their rush for the henhouse, as they spied "Putt-putter," a more terrifying, gigantic hawk than they had ever seen before. We dipped our wings in friendly salute to farmers waving hats as we passed over.

Our pace seemed to slacken as Marvin explained we were coming to some sand hills which demanded more altitude for safe passage. Our climb was only well begun – at 800 feet – when the rough staccato roar of the engine startlingly changed to a half-hearted clatter which one cylinder struggled to maintain. Marvin instantly pulled back the throttle, quickly sized up the wind and the only available field, and we started a gliding turn to the left.

"Can't you make it go?" I asked hopefully, thinking about what a rough landing it would be if we had to put down in the field of foot-deep furrows and ridges below. Marvin opened the throttle wide in a last desperate attempt to continue, but the effort was short-lived as he shook his head and again throttled the engine for our downward plunge. Somewhat to my astonishment, he landed across the ridges instead of taking the smoother course along the ridges. He later explained that in the split-second available, he decided to land into the wind rather than attempt a crosswind landing in which we might have ended on our back. Amazed that the landing was not more violent and the plane was intact, I found my fear of forced landings dissolving. Presence of mind and steady nerves were the only necessities.

Imagine our amusement, several days later, when we had safely flown back to Wichita, to find that a friend had *sent us a clipping with the following glowing newspaper account of the event:*

AIRPLANE FORCED DOWN

"Mr. and Mrs. E.C. Edwards had unexpected guests for dinner Sunday. The plane of Mr. and Mrs. Marvin Michael of Wichita, enroute to St. John to visit his parents, was forced down in the wheat field northwest of the Edwards home, about 11 o'clock. Fortunately the plane landed safely and the occupants were uninjured. The pilot was able to make some mechanical repairs. It was dinner time so Mr. and Mrs. Michael were the guests of the Edwards at dinner. About two o'clock the Michaels were ready to resume their trip. Meanwhile, his father, H.D. Michael of St. John, had driven over to see how serious the accident was, but finding them ready to take to the air again, returned to St. John, taking Mrs. Michael with him. The pilot chose not to risk another forced landing so soon with his recent bride.

"Monday morning about seven o'clock the Michaels passed over the Edwards home on their return trip to Wichita, and signaled the Edwards family with a dip of their wings that everything was fine."

The airport became the center of our leisure activities, with "Putt-putter" taking to the air. Northward we flew one evening in the coolness of approaching dusk, toward Salina. There we met and visited with the members of Indiana (Pa.) State Teachers College summer group on their western tour. On our return trip, savage rain beating relentlessly on red and silver could not diminish our ever-increasing joy of flight.

Kansas was a map at our feet to be explored. Each weekend found us streaking off to some new destination.

Boundless space surrounded us and the steady throb of the engine was music to our ears as we soared high over the heat-scorched plains toward a new quest.

* * * *

Just about the time Laura was becoming adjusted to life in Wichita, Kansas, we decided to move to Burbank, California, where I would be employed by Lockheed. It seemed the right time had come, also, to give up Putt-putter, and I regretfully decided to give some other young fellow the opportunity to know the joy of studying Kansas by air. The wonderful little airplane had certainly fulfilled a rite of passage which would leave me with lifelong memories, but it was time to move on to the next chapter in my life.

En route from Wichita to Burbank, we made a side trip to Seattle, where we were delighted to have dinner with Eddie Allen and his wife. It was great to see him again, and he was interested in hearing about my new job at Lockheed. During dinner he and Florence spoke with great enthusiasm about the dream home which they were building and furnishing in Encinitas, California, where they looked forward to spending their retirement years.

After moving to Burbank, Laura and I took many opportunities for sightseeing in California. On one such venture we stopped at Encinitas, just north of San Diego, hoping to see Eddie Allen's extraordinary house. Mr. Rohn, the caretaker and botanist, greeted us at the door. I explained that I'd worked with Eddie at the Stearman Company. When I mentioned that we'd had dinner with Eddie and Florence in Seattle a year earlier, Mr. Rohn warmed up and invited us in to see the house.

As we entered, he said, "For a good many years now, Eddie's been bringing back unique art treasures from all over the world for his retirement home." Mr. Rohn showed us every room, explaining the Gothic windows, beautiful furniture, the sunken Roman living room. We admired the huge fireplace, the many original paintings and statues from Italy, India, and other places. We climbed the steep, winding staircase stopping to look at all the framed art along the way. Even the bannister, made of intricately carved wood and wrought iron, was a work of art. At the top we opened the door to a solarium filled with blooming roses, geraniums and begonias.

We sat on the rattan furniture enjoying the view. From the top of the cliff one hundred feet above the ocean, we had a 180 degree view of pounding surf, rockstrewn beach and passing ships on the horizon. There in the sunshine, I was taken with this definition of success. I too wanted an opulent house with expensive art work. I wanted to be a millionaire and fly my own airplane everywhere. Laura and I went home full of dreams for our future.

Months later, my hands shook with excitement as I tore open a letter from Eddie Allen at Boeing in Seattle. I wondered what he could be writing me about.

"We are expanding our flight department and have an opening for a combination aerodynamicist and flight test engineer. We can offer $250 a month." (Signed) Edmund T. Allen, Chief of Flight and Aerodynamics.

I couldn't imagine this incredible wealth—more money than I'd ever made, and the opportunity to work with Eddie Allen, my hero. I was ecstatic, but Laura, who had become accustomed to sunny California weather, said, "I don't want to move to Seattle. It rains all the time." After we talked it over, she said, "I guess this will be all right. I know how important it is to you." I threw my arms around her and gave her a big kiss. We gave notice to our apartment manager and packed up our household items. Four weeks later we were in Seattle and I went to work with Eddie Allen. I was thrilled beyond measure to start flying immediately as a flight test engineer, helping to accomplish high altitude tests on the B-17 Flying Fortress.

Chapter Six

FLYING BLIND

By 1940 commercial aviation was booming. Boeing ushered in the four-engine era with its pressurized cabin Stratoliner service from New York to Los Angeles. But the war in Europe changed the aircraft industry's emphasis to military production. In addition to the satisfaction of working closely with Eddie Allen, I enjoyed the challenge of helping Boeing meet the increasing demands being placed upon it. There was a tremendous need for bigger and better planes, and the tests which our department conducted were vital to that effort. The Army Air Corps awarded Boeing an $8 million contract for the B-17C Flying Fortress.

During our first year in Seattle, Laura and I were busy getting our home established, and we were thrilled to be expecting our first child.

I met many new and interesting associates through my work. One of them was Bill Milliken, who was a senior flight test engineer. I was a junior flight test engineer and Bill was my boss. He owned a small airplane, as I formerly had, and this seemed to form a bond between us. We experienced the satisfaction of completing test flights on the huge Boeing bombers, but we also knew the utter joy of flying one-to-one with the elements and observing the countryside from the birdseye view of the small plane.

In October 1941 Bill had a little time off from work and piloted his Fairchild 22, a 90-horsepower two-seater, across the continent to visit his home town in Maine. The airplane had been built in 1933, and had an old-fashioned open cockpit. The meteorology books agreed that prevailing winds always blow from west to east, and Bill counted on this boost to help in his cross-country jaunt. What he encountered instead of helpful tailwinds, however, was six days of east to west headwinds. He averaged 512 miles a day, about 100 miles a day less than he could have achieved by driving a modern car. His time away from work was running out, so he had to leave his plane at an airfield near Boston, 3115 miles from Seattle, and fly home on a commercial airliner.

He had a sad story to relate about bucking those headwinds, but he also had a proposition to make. He would pay my airfare to Boston, if I'd like to go back and pick up the Fairchild for him. "It should be a cinch for you," he said, "now that we know the winds actually are blowing from east to west. Those tailwinds will just naturally carry you all the way back home. I just wish I could do it, but I can't take any more time off."

I had a little time coming from Boeing, and the prospect of a paid trip to Boston and an enjoyable return flight in a small plane appealed to me. When I approached Laura about my wish to make the the trip, she posed no objections. I wasn't too concerned that it was now October. We were having a mild fall in Seattle, and it seemed a little early for heavy winter weather on the east coast. I did realize, however, that it would probably be pretty cold in the open cockpit.

I mentioned that problem over lunch with Eddie Allen. Many years earlier Eddie had been a pioneer airmail pilot, carrying the mail in an open cockpit biplane over the Rockies in all kinds of weather. "Marvin," he said, "I have a flying suit that I wore when I was flying the airmail. It's lined with bear fur, and it's quite warm. Would you like to use it?"

"Would I! That sounds like just the ticket."

I was elated as I boarded a United DC-3 for my first transcontinental airline flight. Deplaning in Boston the next day, I was more tired than elated. I checked into a hotel for a few hours' fitful sleep. Mid afternoon I looked over the Fairchild.

It would be foolhardy to start off across the continent in a small plane I had never flown without first making a thorough checkout. I flew it locally for half an hour, scrutinizing the instruments and gauges. It was shipshape. I was delighted with its maneuverability and better-than-expected visibility from the cockpit.

Back at the hotel, I went over the charts and made out my flight plan for the next day. I turned in early for a good night's sleep.

Next morning at the airport I donned Eddie's flying suit and stuffed my duffel bag in the plane's baggage compartment. I ran up the engine, adjusted my helmet and goggles, and was off and climbing out to the west.

Navigation in the eastern states is more difficult than in Kansas or Washington, where I had done most of my flying. The roads in Kansas (and to a lesser extent in Washington) run east, west, north or south. Holding a course is easy. Back east, where the roads run in all directions, I had to set up a precise compass course and keep comparing landmarks against the map to check sideways wind drift.

The cities are close together and look very much alike from the air. Just when you think you've identified one city, you approach the next. Hey, this is great, I thought as I crossed the five long narrow finger lakes in central New York state. They are an unmistakable aid to navigation, but the headwinds were so strong I only got as far as Buffalo, New York. Only 450 miles the first day! So far I was even behind the 512 miles Bill Milliken had averaged.

The next morning I was grounded by low clouds and restricted visibility. I didn't feel free to go sightseeing in Buffalo—it just might clear up.

Second day, more of the same. It sure got boring sitting in the terminal reading magazines, walking over to the window and checking the weather every little bit. Most pilots are impatient and I'm no exception. Frustrated, I recalled the old saying, "If you have time to spare, go by air."

On the third day my chafing ended abruptly when by midmorning the clouds had lifted and flying conditions reached acceptable minimums. Once more I climbed into my bear suit and took off. Fidgety to make up for lost time, I flew above scattered clouds until they became broken. The forecaster had said, "You'll have good weather all the way to Erie," and I foolishly believed him.

Before long the clouds rose beneath, forcing me to climb up into the cold air above them. I shivered as the freezing blast chilled me, fur suit notwithstanding. I began to understand why bears find a cozy cave in which to hibernate in the winter. Time dragged. The broken clouds became a solid overcast. All I could do now was hold a steady compass course. Fortunately the air was smooth so the compass didn't bounce around.

What if the forecaster were wrong and I had to let down through this stuff without blind flying instruments? I knew the ceiling was low, which meant that I could fly right into hills, trees or buildings. What if a crosswind blew me out over Lake Erie and the engine quit? What if, what if, what if? My apprehension mounted by the minute.

Shivering uncontrollably, I thought of Laura, my pregnant wife. What would happen to her if I didn't make it? Why did I ever let myself get into this mess? Dear God, if you help me out of this one, I'll never, ever get myself in a pickle like this again.

Because the engine exhaust stacks were so short in the Fairchild, the staccato roar of the engine was exceptionally loud. It was getting on my nerves, and certainly added to my fatigue. I thought about my continuing dream of owning my own airplane again, and I made a mental note that an enclosed heated cabin would certainly be an important requirement. (We didn't wear ear plugs in those days when flying, but after jets came in, we were glad to wear them.)

I had been flying almost five hours, but it seemed an eternity. The long flight in the small plane was possible only because of the reliable old Cirrus engine and the auxiliary fuel tank Bill had installed in the forward cockpit. At last I spotted a tiny hole in the clouds below. It was too small to safely descend through, but I was cautiously optimistic there soon would be larger holes.

None appeared. Should I have tried descending through that tiny hole? I could never go back now and find it. The engine droned on. Hey! A little hole and then another. Thank God! Anxious to end the ordeal, I picked one that was none too large.

I throttled back and as the engine purred softly it was a tremendous relief to be free of the noise and to know that after all my very real concerns I was going to be safe. I circled down through the hole and spotted the ground! The tension vanished immediately and a great weight lifted from my shoulders.

The area below was more heavily populated than central New York. But where was I? Ten minutes, then twenty slipped by as I studied the landscape and compared it with the map. To the north was a body of water that had to be Lake Erie. In the distance to the northwest was a large city, which I needed to identify as soon as possible. Turning toward it, I soon determined it was Toledo, Ohio. Hooray! I was very nearly on course. I quickly selected a new heading for my destination: Ann Arbor, Michigan. After four hours and 41 minutes I landed at Ann Arbor, extremely tired, and relieved to be back at the University of Michigan.

The next day sped by as I revisited my alma mater. One of my former professors, E.W. Conlon, invited me to stay overnight with his family. By the time I'd wound up my visit I made a late takeoff at 2:30 p.m. Two and a half hours later I saw in the distance factories with tall smokestacks belching clouds of smoke. It looked like it might be Gary, Indiana, a city I had hitchhiked through on my way to the University of Michigan.

Fifteen minutes more. Still more heavily populated to the north. Oh no! It has to be Chicago! I couldn't land at the big Chicago airport without radio. I was bone tired. It was getting late, and a thick haze limited the visibility. But suddenly I spotted what appeared to be an airport up ahead. Drawing closer, I saw planes parked near a hangar, and an airplane taking off. Was I in luck! I entered the traffic pattern and landed, taxied to a gas pump and cut the switch. As the attendant approached I asked, "Where am I?"

With a quizzical smile he answered, "Wheaton. Where'd you come from?"

"Ann Arbor, Michigan." After an uneventful overnight, I headed west next morning.

Except for headwinds, things went smoothly as far as Minnesota. I was running behind schedule and anxious to get home. Weather was clear, so I pushed on beyond my anticipated stopover even though it was late afternoon. The wind usually dies down late in the day, but not this day.

It began to get dark. Still fighting a strong headwind, I suddenly realized it would be quite dark by the time I reached my next intended destination. Furthermore, it would be difficult to locate a strange airport in the fast-fading twilight. I began looking for a pasture big enough and smooth enough to land in.

At last I spotted one that looked OK. I circled, gradually losing altitude as I studied the terrain. I made a low pass, pulled up, and made my landing approach. About to touch down, it seemed much darker than I expected. I felt a brief panic, but it would only be darker if I went around again, so I gritted my teeth and felt my way down. I bounced, but not too badly, and rolled to a stop. What a comfort to be on solid ground!

Cautiously I taxied up to a fence and shut down the engine. With a rope from the baggage compartment I tied the plane to a couple of fence posts, then with duffel bag in hand, I walked toward a farmhouse I had seen from the air. Halfway there, I spied a man approaching. He wore a blue denim workshirt and overalls. His weatherbeaten face and gnarled hands told me life on the farm was not easy. I judged he was in his fifties. He introduced himself as Hank Weaver, and inquired anxiously, "Are you OK?"

"Yeah. I got caught by the dark and had to land while I could still see. How far is it into town?"

"About eight miles."

"Is there a hotel in town?"

"Not really." After a moment's hesitation, "You could stay with us—nothin' fancy."

On the plains of Minnesota airplanes still aroused curiosity. Relieved by his invitation, I readily accepted. Midwest country folks were more hospitable than city people. We were greeted in the house by a smiling woman in a blue and white print housedress. "Here's my wife, Nancy," he said.

"Pleased to meet you. It's late; you must be real hungry. I'll warm up some vittles."

She set some warmed up leftovers before me and poured a cup of coffee.

"Where ya' headed for?" Mr. Weaver asked.

"Seattle."

"You don't say—you got a fur piece to go."

A little more small talk and we all retired early. I awoke next morning to the welcome smell of frying bacon and coffee. A hearty breakfast of hot biscuits, bacon, eggs, fried potatoes, coffee, and I was ready to go. "How much do I owe you?" I asked.

"Not a thing," was Weaver's reply.

I offered him a bill but he refused it.

"Aw, no. We was glad to have you."

I thanked them, shook hands, and started toward the plane.

"Here, climb in the pickup and I'll run you out there." I protested but he insisted. He watched, curious, as I completed my daily preflight check. Another handshake and I climbed in and took off.

One week, 255 gallons of gas, ten quarts of oil and many hours of generally miserable flying conditions later, I landed in Seattle. Yes, you know the story. The winds had reversed and I too bucked headwinds from coast to coast. Bill Milliken was delighted to get his airplane back in the northwest. He expressed his regret that the tailwinds he had promised would waft me across the continent had failed to do so. We agreed that changes needed to be made in those meteorology textbooks concerning prevailing winds.

The memory of those bone-chilling hours in an open cockpit and the deafening engine exhaust was like a bad dream. They say suffering builds character, but I knew I never again wanted to go through an experience like that. One thing for sure: I learned to know my piloting limitations and I vowed to stay within them for the rest of my flying days.

Marvin Michael zips oxygen bailout bottle in place
before entering low pressure chamber for training
"flight." 1940

Chapter Seven

ASK AND YOU
SHALL RECEIVE

The war intensified. Two German U-boats were being sunk each day along our East Coast and in the Gulf of Mexico. The war in the Pacific was going badly. Boeing opened additional plants in Seattle, Renton, and Wichita, and the Army ordered 250 B-29 Superfortress bombers. Almost a fifth of Seattle's population was involved with Boeing work, either directly or through subcontractors. The pre-war assembly line had been essentially a male stronghold, but now more and more women went to work for Boeing. Eventually women made up 46 percent of the Boeing workforce.

The experimental flight test department was working every day, seventy hours a week. I paid little attention to my family, determined to make my mark in the world. Boeing routinely got occupational deferments for employees considered vital to the war effort. The stress of the lengthy work week began to take its toll, and I was weary. I asked the Boeing flight physician if he could recommend to my boss that I take a week off to rest, and he obliged.

I needed to think through a monumental problem that was troubling me. Could I become a test pilot? As a flight test engineer on B-17 Flying Fortress flights, I stood behind the pilot and copilot while with intense concentration and lightning speed I recorded altitude, airspeed, outside air temperature, power settings and many other data.

The Boeing flight test section was expanding rapidly. Young test pilots were being hired who I felt were less qualified than myself, and I thought this might be my opportunity to become a test pilot. These wet-behind-the-ears young fellows were for the most part recent engineering graduates, while I had completed my master's degree four years earlier. In the interim, I had worked most of the time as a flight test engineer. I already knew the B-17. I had a practical working knowledge of the takeoff and climb speeds, the landing approach speed, the sound of the engines in these realms of flight, and a lot more. I was frustrated that Boeing was hiring these young engineers with much less experience than I had, to do the job I wanted. Tired, confused, and emotional, I made plans to go camping alone so I could think out what I needed to do.

Soon I was trudging up the Dosewallops River trail with a heavy pack of camping gear. The Olympic mountains, west of Seattle, were strikingly beautiful. Dose Meadows was a riot of color; daisies, blue lupin, fireweed and many other wildflowers blanketed the landscape. It was quiet, the silence broken only by the sweet songs of birds and the whistling marmots. It was the perfect place to think. I was desperately afraid my boss, the chief test pilot, would not agree that I was as well or better qualified than the new hires. I wrote down every conceivable question the boss might ask me, and then wrote my response. I put labeled thumb tabs on the pages so I could turn quickly to the right answer. Feeling good and with a lighter pack, I headed for home.

Back in the office, I made an appointment to see the boss. Trembling inwardly with apprehension, I said, "I've been doing a lot of thinking. I believe I'm better qualified than some of the new pilots you've been hiring." I detailed my proposal.

To my great surprise and delight, he asked no questions but hesitated only a moment and said, "As soon as you find someone to take over your responsibilities you can begin checking out as a pilot." I was elated!

So as it turned out, all I had to do was ask! But thanks to the excellent advice of Eddie Allen, I had prepared myself thoroughly with the engineering skills which led to this next important step in my career. In the 1930's, Hollywood movies had portrayed test pilots as handsome young daredevils wearing helmet, goggles, streaming white silk scarf and handlebar mustache. In reality most of us were of a different breed. "For an engineering test pilot," Eddie Allen once said, "I'd rather have a man with an engineering degree and two hundred hours' flying time than a man with ten thousand hours and no engineering training." That's where I fit in.

There was considerable stress involved in my new role as a test pilot, but also a great deal of enjoyment and the sense of making a real contribution.

As a flight test engineer I had been a valuable member of the flight test team, but now as a pilot I must assume even greater personal responsibility. A lot depended upon the split second decisions I must make from day to day. Boeing was entrusting to me an airplane which represented a tremendous investment of time and money, and which would be vital to the war effort. Even more important, of course, was my duty to protect to the utmost the lives of crew members who flew with me.

Many flight offices display a plaque which reads, "The air, even more than the sea, is unforgiving of errors." Members of the flight test department were concerned—yes, worried...about our security. When Boeing-test pilots began high altitude flight testing in 1940, they entered a new realm never before approached. They flew twice as high as before, and faced many new problems. On becoming a test pilot in 1942, I was fully cognizant of the risks we all must live with. Soberly we recalled the crash several years earlier of the Boeing Stratoliner, with the loss of nine lives. We remembered a Lockheed test pilot whose career ended when his oxygen system failed.

All of us, I'm sure, gave at least occasional thought to how we should or would react in a serious flight emergency. Pondering this, I remembered a *Reader's Digest* article which told of the big game hunting exploits of a man named Carl Ackley. What was it about big game hunting in Africa that I thought could relate to flight testing? It was the plan which Ackley had evolved for dealing with possible life-threatening emergencies in his work. Ackley had this to say: "I had a few close calls which caused me to do some serious thinking. I tried to conceive of every possible emergency, and what I would do to extricate myself. In my imagination an elephant suddenly charged me and I had no time to escape. I figured I'd grab the two tusks and position myself between them until there was a chance to escape.

"One day this actually happened! The furious animal tried to dislodge me, but I maintained a tight grip. Finally, I saw an opportunity to get away. Grabbing an overhead limb of a huge tree, I waited until the elephant was well out of range, then climbed down to safety. I'm sure the elephant would have killed me if I hadn't thought out what I'd do ahead of time."

I told my boss this anecdote and suggested we do a similar thing. He agreed and assigned me to head up the project. We developed a set of High Altitude Flight Test Emergency Procedures. When weather was bad and test flights were not possible, we pilots gathered in a conference room and worked out a course of action for every conceivable emergency. We read all the accident reports put out by the FAA and the Air Force and discussed how we could have prevented them. If an engine were to fail on takeoff, we would set up emergency power on the remaining engines and feather the propeller on the failed engine. If we smelled gasoline fumes in the plane, for the remainder of the flight we would not use any nonessential piece of electrical equipment that could spark an explosion.

To put this in perspective, the first 25 years of aviation history constitute an era of remarkable accomplishments by pioneering individuals, beginning with the Wright Brothers' flight at Kitty Hawk in 1903 and ending with the transatlantic flight of Charles Lindbergh. But it was the second 25 years when the groundwork was laid for progress which led from the wood-framed, fabric-covered biplanes to the mature, commercial means of transportation we know today, the sweptwing jet.

In 1940, airliners cruised at 15,000 feet or less. However, the Bell and the Curtiss aircraft companies were flying experimental single-seater fighter planes to 35,000 feet, where the pilots leveled off for a short time and then went back to land. But Boeing was the real pioneer in high altitude flight test research. We in the Boeing flight test department were the first to take six or eight crewmen to 40,000 feet or more. Bell and Curtiss pilots stayed at altitude just minutes; only the exterior metal skin got cold. We flew at altitude for four or five hours at temperatures as low as 125 degrees Fahrenheit below zero. Much of the interior structure got thoroughly cold-soaked. In 1940, fighter planes had a shorter mission and didn't need to carry enough fuel to stay up as long as the bombers.

In one lengthy flight at high altitude, I discovered the flight controls had become mushy and ineffective. When I called for aileron, rudder or elevator movement, the plane's response was seriously delayed.

Turning to my copilot I said, "Jim, feel these controls. Something's haywire."

Jim gingerly tested the wheel and rudder pedals and said, "You're right. This could give us some real trouble when we come in for landing." We completed the test as planned and full of apprehension, began our descent. On our return to the field, we cautiously monitored the situation. Strangely, some of the looseness disappeared, but I made a bone-jarring landing.

"Whew! That was a close one!" I said, relieved and grateful to be safe on the ground.

We described the phenomenon to the Project Engineers. They studied the data and eventually explained our problem. Structures engineer Ted Blomquist said,

"The fuselage is aluminum alloy and the cables are steel. As the plane became cold-soaked, the aluminum framework shrank more than the steel cables, and the cables became floppy. When Marv moved the controls, they took up the slack before starting to move the control surfaces."

The engineers designed and installed tension regulators to keep the cables tight at all temperatures so the airplane response would be more positive. We tested them and reported that they had corrected the problem.

Another difficulty test pilot Elliott Merrill and I encountered during a flight concerned the propeller governors which kept the props turning at constant speed. After three hours of flying at high altitude, the number two engine suddenly oversped. The noise was deafening and frightened us badly. My heart raced and I was sure the plane was going to disintegrate. But Elliott, in the left seat, immediately throttled back the engine. "Wow!" Elliott exclaimed, "Wonder what caused that!" We studied the instruments.

"I don't see anything that could have caused it," I said. Our jangled nerves quieted down after a few minutes.

Elliott asked, "Marv, do you see any reason why we can't just nurse this engine along and go ahead with our flight?" I agreed and we resumed our test. Suddenly number three engine oversped, and again Elliott throttled it back quickly.

We immediately discontinued testing and Elliott called Boeing Radio, "Our engines are overspeeding and we're coming in. Call Powerplant and get Bob Jewett to come to our postflight conference."

We landed and adjourned to the meeting room. A stenotypist recorded everything as we explained to Jewett what had happened. He pondered the problem. Finally he said, "I can't see any reason for this. I'll go along on your next flight to observe."

On the succeeding flight he was still mystified. He observed the governors as the hydraulic pressure changed the pitch of the propellers. He finally concluded, "After a long cold-soak at altitude, the hydraulic oil congealed and stopped flowing. This allowed the propeller to go into flat pitch and caused the engines to overspeed. As you found out, it's like driving along and suddenly shifting into low gear. This is potentially a very dangerous situation. As you know, this happens so fast that if Elliott hadn't throttled back immediately, the overspeeding would have caused the engine to disintegrate. It could have wrenched the engine right out of the plane, and you could have lost control."

Jewett had the mechanics drill a small hole in the propeller dome so the warm hydraulic oil could slowly bleed through the system and prevent congealing. On our third flight we again experienced overspeeding, but it wasn't as bad as before.

This time we drilled a larger hole, but on the fourth flight the RPM wouldn't hold constant. It kept oscillating above and below the desired RPM. For the fifth flight we drilled a hole intermediate in size and it worked fine.

Sometimes I've been asked if we crew members were nervous about making subsequent flights in attempts to find a solution for a fairly frightening problem we had earlier encountered. We of course would have no guarantee that the problem might not occur on the following flight as well. I always explained that we placed great faith in the training we had received in how to deal with the unexpected.

We Boeing pilots undoubtedly saved lives by following Carl Ackley's example in working out a course of action for every possible emergency. The steps we took gave us the confidence to accept calculated risks in an occupation known to be hazardous. It is gratifying to know that now all pilots' flight manuals have emergency procedure checklists.

Pilots and crew prepare by breathing pure oxygen to relieve nitrogen from blood. 1941

Boeing B-17 Flying Fortress. 1942

Chapter Eight

THE WORLD'S GREATEST TEST PILOT

Through the years he was my role model. If I could be a reasonably good test pilot and have a fraction of Eddie Allen's understanding, sympathy, and patience, I'd be happy. *Time* magazine's description of him as "the greatest test pilot aviation has ever had," fell far short of describing the man he really was. He could converse for hours on astronomy, constellations, Italian art, the Taj Mahal, world travels. He kept listeners spellbound, reciting long ballads from memory.

I felt safer flying with Eddie than with any other pilot. The insurance companies shared my confidence in his skill, for they offered Douglas, Lockheed and other manufacturers substantially lower rates if Eddie, rather than any other pilot, made the initial flight on a new model. I couldn't help feeling Eddie was just about infallible. Eddie's Air Medal simply confirmed it for me:

THE WHITE HOUSE
CITATION FOR AIR MEDAL

Mr. Edmund T. Allen, Civilian Test Pilot. For meritorious achievement in aerial flight on 30 December 1942. On this occasion while piloting an Army Air Forces XB-29 aircraft, under extremely unfavorable flying conditions, an uncontrollable fire developed in the No. 4 engine. In spite of the fact that he would have been justified in abandoning the airplane under such conditions, Mr. Allen elected to remain at the controls and attempt to safely land it. As a result of his skill and daring, invaluable test data and a prototype airplane were saved, the loss of which would have immeasurably retarded the entire B-29 program at a crucial time in its development.

(Signed) Harry Truman

In 1943 the German army was rolling over Europe, and the U.S. Air Force was anxiously awaiting a new long-range plane which Boeing would deliver shortly. Eddie Allen was completing tests on the XB-29 Superfortress, a highly advanced supersecret four-engine bomber. (The X designated the plane as experimental.)

On the morning of February 18, 1943, Eddie took the XB-29 on a test flight, knowing that the plane was not airworthy. It was powered by the Wright 18-cylinder R-3350 engines which were of recent design. On average, an engine was replaced every week on the XB-

29 due to failure. But Eddie knew the Air Force was pressuring Boeing to accelerate delivery of thousands of B-29 Superfortresses, which were desperately needed in the Pacific to turn the tide of war. Never before had an airplane been ordered into such large scale production without a prototype being built and tested. Boeing's reputation warranted the exception. So much depended upon this airplane that Eddie felt compelled to take a calculated risk.

He headed south on leaving Boeing Field, and shortly after takeoff a fire started in engine No. 2, which the flight engineer put out with the built-in fire extinguisher. In making an emergency return to the field, Eddie chose to fly a wide downwind leg over Lake Washington rather than risk a downwind landing in an unfamiliar, untested airplane. During the process a second fire broke out which could not be extinguished.

Black smoke trailed from the plane as it dropped ever lower, flying more rapidly than normal. It headed straight for the Frye meat packing plant, about a mile north of Boeing Field. At 12:23 p.m. the XB-29 struck power lines near the plant, causing lightning-like flashes and cutting off power over a wide area. Then the plane crashed into Frye's and exploded. The flight had lasted just 18 minutes.

Some Frye employees were eating lunch. Others were working in the hog-killing room. Flames shot high in the air. Human screams and the frantic squealing of trapped hogs were heard over the roar of the fire. The eleven crew members were killed, as were twenty-one persons on the ground.

If the fire had rekindled two minutes earlier, they likely could have ditched in the lake with little or no loss of life. If it had broken out two minutes later they would have been safe on Boeing Field. Alternately, a downwind landing choice would surely have been successful.

At the Boeing plant, the rumor spread quickly that Eddie had crashed and was believed killed in the XB-29. When the news reached the flight test department we didn't believe it. I ran to the window. It couldn't be Eddie—somehow he would survive. Yet there was the tall plume of black smoke up north where the plane was thought to have crashed.

After what seemed an unbearably long time, Eddie's secretary came out of her office and sobbed, "Yes, it *was* Eddie." I was stunned, crushed, paralyzed. Eddie couldn't be dead! We pulled our chairs in a circle and asked how this could have happened.

Boeing Vice-president Wellwood Beall asked Sid Silber, a flight test engineer, and me to go to the morgue and assist in identifying the bodies, which left me with an indelible memory of the horror of the crash. Ed Wersbe and Chuck Blaine had bailed out at 300 feet, too low for their chutes to open. Their injuries were so severe that we had difficulty being sure of their identity. We were then asked to identify the body they suspected was Eddie Allen's. His features were so badly burned that we had to say we couldn't be certain of his identity.

I was devastated by Eddie's tragic death. He was only forty-seven. I knew all of the eleven crew members well, and five of them were especially close friends. We'd worked and played together for years. Chuck Blaine was one of the five. He was greatly loved by his co-workers, and had a happy smile for everyone. For the longest week of my life, Laura and I spent most of our time helping Chuck's family with final arrangements. This Boeing assignment enabled me to do a little something worthwhile during a time when I was unable to concentrate on any engineering work.

The sight of eleven flag-draped caskets banked with flowers at the memorial service in the Masonic Temple brought intense anguish. I struggled to hold back tears throughout the service. The friend and mentor whom I idolized was dead. Boeing briefly halted work in tribute to the employees who had lost their lives, as the plant's loudspeakers carried the bugler's "Taps" from the Masonic Temple.

The names of the eleven men are inscribed on a memorial plaque in downtown Seattle, along with those of service personnel who died for their country. The lives of Eddie Allen and his crew were as much a wartime sacrifice as any of those which were lost in distant battle zones. When Boeing inaugurated its new $750,000 wind tunnel the following year, it was named the Edmund T. Allen Memorial Aeronautical Laboratories.

Laura and I recalled sadly our visit to Eddie's "castle," perched on the bluff overlooking the blue Pacific. We were filled with regret that he had been denied the happy retirement years he looked forward to spending there.

As the pain and grief slowly eased in the following weeks and months, I realized that the best way for me to reconstruct my shattered world was to carry on the unfinished task, endeavoring to follow in Eddie's footsteps as closely as possible. This in itself would be "the grand struggle against big odds toward an achievement," of which he had made me aware so long ago in his inspiring letter.

Test pilot Marvin Michael awaits word the airplane
is ready to go. 1943

Chapter Nine

A BUSMAN'S HOLIDAY

The Boeing Seattle plant was feverishly working around the clock in 1943, rolling a dozen bombers out the door every day. The flight test chief, lean and thoughtful N. D. Showalter, agreed when Doc Russell, the flight test physician insisted, "Two years of hitting the ball day and night, Sundays and holidays, is too much exacting work without a break. Fitzpatrick and Michael absolutely must take a couple of weeks off if they keep flight testing those birds up to 35,000 feet every day."

"Why not take a busman's holiday and fly a light plane to Mexico?" I suggested to John Fitzpatrick. "That would be a lead pipe cinch for relaxation after flying B-17's all the time."

Pat's flight test engineer job and my work as test pilot had long since shown us that the glamorous, happy-go-lucky days of flying had gone out with the Lindberghs and the barnstormers of the Twenties. Our flight to Mexico would just be a restful way of utilizing our workaday knowledge to cover 5,600 miles in two weeks, without taxing wartime travel facilities.

Piloting our flying club's little red, high-wing Stinson was uneventful until we reached Texas. After landing at Laredo Army Air Field, Pat and I rode in a jeep to the Base Operations office. We were apprehensive because we knew only too well that private planes had no business landing here. Yet our Foreign Flight Authorization plainly stated we were cleared to fly across the border at Laredo. We couldn't help it if there was no civilian airport in town. Foolish to worry though, for the Army was very cooperative, and promptly phoned customs officials to help speed us on our way to Mexico City.

After making the call, however, Captain Berdines Lackness, operations officer at Laredo, gave us the sad news. "They seem to have made a mistake in your papers in Washington, D.C.. You'll have to fly to Brownsville to cross the border. Only commercial planes can cross over here at Laredo."

"Just wait," Pat said to me. "We'll land in a Mexican clink yet."

We took off for Brownsville, munching cookies and candy as we soared over endless orange groves. Pat mused, "Wonder how N.D. and the boys in Seattle are doing on the pressure survey B-29. They ought to move Boeing Flight Test to Texas if the weather here is always this good." Pat was not a pilot, so I made all the takeoffs and landings, but he flew the plane some of the time, just to relieve me.

After landing at Brownsville we agreed that our map situation needed prompt attention. During wartime the military was very stingy with maps of foreign countries. Now we really needed a reliable map to get us into Mexico. In desperation I phoned an acquaintance, Steve

Kitchell, with Pan American Airways in Brownsville, who agreed to get us some maps.

Early the next morning we stripped everything from the plane that could possibly be left behind, since we didn't want to hinder the ability of our 80 hp Stinson 10A to climb over the highest peaks. We removed sleeping bags, heavy underwear, hand axe and the empty third seat, then started in on the paper work.

As requested in our Foreign Flight Authorization, I notified the clearing station officer of Air Transport Command, Brownsville Municipal Airport, Brownsville, Texas, and the commanding officer of Naval Air Station, Corpus Christi, Texas, as to the purpose of our flight, time and date of departure from Brownsville, proposed itinerary, identification of the aircraft, and names and citizenship of persons carried therein.

At Brownsville the clearing station officer, Lt. McCormick, briefed me for the flight to Mexico.

"On the hop to Tampico," he advised, "follow the coastline. If you have to make a forced landing, you can set down on the hard, wet sand along the water's edge. Don't land on the dry sand farther inland. From the air it looks hard and smooth, but it's actually soft, full of dunes, and covered with driftwood."

Pat flew the plane down the coast to Tampico while I blissfully wrote postcards. Soon after we refueled and took off from Tampico, we encountered problems from which we surmised that private flying isn't always the cut and dried business we had thought. There were very few roads, railroads, cities and other landmarks between Tampico and Mexico City by which a pilot could positively determine his location. Our maps showed little detail, and we discovered later they were marked, "Advance proof—subject to correction." From Brownsville to Tampico our compass had been in error about 18 degrees. We made allowance for this error as we headed for Mexico City, but it later appeared that our compass had begun to read correctly some time after leaving Tampico.

Billowing cumulus clouds stretched out their fleecy arms to engulf us, so Pat shouted above the roar of the engine, "Why don't we climb on top, Mike?"

I balked. I was sure those towering clouds extended upwards 16,000 to 18,000 feet. Our unsupercharged engine was in for a struggle just to climb 11,000 feet over the rim of the Sierra Oriental, northeast of Mexico City. A mechanic in Brownsville had been the first to tell us our radio would be of no help in navigating Mexico's shaggy terrain. "Your radio is low frequency, and the Mexican radio range stations are all high frequency," he said. There went our plans for riding the beam into Mexico City. As we approached the mountain tops the clouds edged in closer as though determined to block our every avenue of escape. We threaded our way up a deep narrow canyon. Occasional glimpses of blue sky beckoned us onward, offering hope that our little plane could climb through. As we neared the hole, however, it proved to be so high above us that we had to circle for about ten minutes to gain altitude.

I was piloting the plane at this time and was sitting on the edge of my seat with my hand ready to jam the throttle wide open if we came too close for comfort to the clouds or the canyon wall. When another opening at a lower altitude became visible, we darted for it before it could disappear. Breaking over the canyon rim, we flew at rooftop height over the hut of a startled-looking Mexican. I could imagine his astonishment as we fanned the soot off his chimney.

The weather was better up on the plateau, but the clouds still obscured distant objects. Despite our concentrated efforts, we were unable to identify any of the small villages over which we flew. We circled a fair-sized city three times, studying intently its railroad and other features in a vain effort to identify it. Just to the west, a welcome sight came into view—a flat, grassy field with a conspicuous white circle in the center identifying it as an airport. There were no buildings or facilities. We later learned that it was a military emergency field. We landed the plane, hoping there would be someone around to tell us where we were. The landing speed was substantially higher at the 8,000 foot elevation, and we used up a lot of runway before rolling to a stop. We didn't dare shut down the engine, as it might be difficult to restart it at the high altitude.

I jumped out of the plane and then stood open-mouthed as hundreds of excited, shouting Mexicans surged across the airport toward us.

"Holy mackeral," I yelled, "Where'd they all come from?"

They were clamoring all around me now. Furiously turning the pages of my vest-pocket Spanish dictionary, I tried to recall my two years of high school Spanish. I shouted above the sound of the engine, jabbing my finger at the map. "Donde estamos?" I asked. I was positive that was correct for "Where are we?" But they only stared blankly at me. I became anxiously aware that the Mexicans were rapidly surrounding the entire airplane. I retreated hastily to the cockpit, set the parking brake, and yelled to Pat, "Get in front of the plane and keep them from dashing their brains out in the propeller."

He accomplished this with great difficulty, and said later, "I was scared to death they would keep on crowding and push *me* into the prop!"

Finally the Mexicans grasped our need to know where we had landed, and they shouted, "Apizaco!" pointing to its location on our map, fifty miles east of Mexico City. Waving them back with "Muchas gracias," I called Pat and we were on our way—for a few brief minutes.

As I opened the throttle the plane accelerated lazily, the engine gasping for breath in the thin air at 8,000 feet. I had to swerve sharply to miss the scores of people who started to run in front of us as we took off. When we were moving too fast to throttle back and stop, I realized to my great dismay that we were not going to clear the telephone wires at the end of the field. The Mexicans and a stone wall confronted us on the right, and we were too low to swing left over the cemetery which bordered the field.

As pilots often do, I had planned what I would do if I were ever caught in a situation like this. I would lower the wing flaps at the last instant and zoom over the obstruction. Then I would skim the ground, picking up speed until I could ease the flaps up and start climbing. There came that last split second when the decision could no longer be postponed. I knew beyond all doubt that we had insufficient speed to even attempt the escape maneuver. There was only one possible course of action.

"Pat, we're going under the wires!" I nosed under the first two sets and we cleared a railroad embankment. We went under the third set of wires, but CRUNCH! A fourth set threw us against our safety belts with a sudden terrific jolt. The engine quit abruptly.

The dust flew as the plane stopped with its nose buried in the ground and its tail high in the air.

We scrambled out, congratulating ourselves on escaping without even a scratch. Once again the Mexican multitudes came swarming around the plane. Pat was mumbling again about the clink in which we would probably end up, charged with severing the town's communications. With forced nonchalance I snapped several pictures of the undignified position in which our little red plane now reposed. I asked Pat to keep the people off the airplane while I telephoned Mexico City regarding our unseemly landing.

Surrounded by chattering men and boys, I set out for town on foot. They talked too fast for me to understand what they were saying. A short way down the road I heard a commotion and turned to investigate. Half walking, half running came a squat figure who was introduced as "El Profesor." He was Professor Procopio Jimenez Lopez—a colorful character we shall long remember. He wore a jaunty cap, and with a friendly smile he enthusiastically offered his services as interpreter. We would never have guessed from his youthful appearance that he had served and been wounded in the Mexican Navy, had been in nearly every country in the world, and spoke Spanish, English, French, Portugese and Italian. He was our constant companion, interpreter, guide, philosopher and entertainer during our stay in his community.

Apizaco was a typical slow-paced Mexican town. The unpaved streets were lined with one story buildings, although its one hotel and a few other buildings were two stories. They were mostly adobe, plastered on the outside and painted a dingy white or pale yellow. El Profesor took me to the telephone office.

I expected to be back at the plane in 40 or 50 minutes, but two hours later I was still trying to get my call through. Meanwhile Pat had become concerned and came looking for me. He entered the telephone office followed closely by an entourage of clamoring Mexican boys who sought his autograph in their school books. After an exasperating three hours I finally completed the call.

While we waited to complete my call, Pat began to fidget. He whispered something to El Profesor, who responded, "Sure. Come on—we go to de Palacio Municipal." They crossed the street and entered the City Hall, where they were ushered through empty jail rooms. El Profesor pointed to a door marked "Senores," and Pat entered.

As Pat started to rejoin El Profesor, he realized his worse fears. The jailer had securely locked him behind bars. Although he could hear voices, not a soul was in sight.

"Hey Profesor!" he bellowed.

El Profesor came down the corridor as fast as his stubby legs would carry him. "What's de matter?" he asked, and then seeing a worried Pat on the other side of the bars, he grasped the situation. "Oh, dey lock you in! Just a minute—I get you out."

As the jailer unlocked the door, El Profesor explained to Pat, "Eet was a meesunderstanding. He thought you are supposed to be put in jail. Eet's a good tink I'm here to feex everyting up for you."

As Pat related the incident to me he moaned, "I knew I'd end up in a Mexican jail sooner or later."

In the Hotel Imperial cafe, the waiter asked us in Spanish what we wanted to eat. Apparently my high school Spanish left a lot to be desired, for the waiter brought each of us a cup of hot milk instead of the coffee I thought I had ordered. Somehow we got through to him, and my mistake was remedied when he set before us a small vinegar jug full of a potent-looking black liquid which proved to be 100-octane coffee.

The next morning the two famous 17,500-foot volcanic peaks, Popocatepetl and Ixtacihuatl, greeted our eyes in all their snowcapped majesty. We agreed they were making their appearance a little too late; if these towering, distinctive peaks had not been obscured by cumulus the previous day, we would never have become lost.

An eager Mexican boy about fifteen-years-old helped us remove the wings and fragile instruments from the plane. A survey of the damage showed that the propeller, nose section and a wing tip were broken. Otherwise it was in good shape. When El Profesor and I had arranged with local truckers to haul the plane to Mexico City, everybody wanted to help us load. We told them we could pay only three, but many more than the appointed three jumped in with gusto to help. When the job was done, all the Mexicans in the countryside clamored for money, but we kept our word and paid only the selected three.

We headed for a repair shop in Mexico City. I kept looking back anxiously to see if the plane was still there. In Mexico City we phoned N.D. Showalter to obtain a wartime airline priority, and were able to buy tickets to get home.

On our flight back to Seattle, Pat and I had time to ponder about just where our carefree vacation had gone astray. We recalled the circumstances of our downfall, and decided that none of them had been our fault. If the compass had not been erratic, if the weather had been only enough better to see Popocatepetl and Ixtacihuatl, if the maps had shown more detail or been a little more accurate, if Mexican radio ranges had been low-frequency instead of high-frequency, if the altitude at Apizaco had been a little lower, the airstrip had been a little longer, the cemetery had been located elsewhere, the telephone wires had been a little higher or lower or fewer, or the crowds of Mexicans had not swarmed in front of us as we attempted our takeoff, we would never have interrupted the Apizaco telephone service!

But memory has softened the more painful aspects of our trip. Had our vacation turned out just as planned, we would not have experienced the enjoyment of mingling with native Mexicans in picturesque rural Apizaco, we would not have encountered our charming friend, El Profesor, and Pat would not have been locked up in a Mexican jail. A spirit of adventure and the somewhat unpredictable nature of flying a small plane opened our eyes to enchanting new lands we'll never forget.

Chapter Ten

THIS WAY OUT

On March 13, 1943, my fellow test pilot for the day's project was Elliott Merrill. He was under 40, and had taught hundreds of students to fly. I felt comfortable on Elliott's team, having experienced a number of emergencies with him which I felt he handled with skill and confidence. A few months earlier, an engine oversped on a flight over Bellingham. The propeller governor failed, and the rpm climbed explosively—a potentially dangerous situation. The roar of the engine and propeller startled me, but Elliott quickly and calmly throttled back, so that the engine didn't self-destruct.

Today as Elliott and I drove from the office to the flight test hangar on the other side of Boeing Field, he commented on the dozens of giant barrage balloons which floated high in the sky, tethered to the ground by heavy cables.

"I wonder how effective they would really be in keeping the Jap planes from dive bombing Boeing," said Elliott. "I don't know," I replied, "but the balloons at least would keep them high enough to destroy their accuracy."

The possibility of air strikes by the Japanese was a very real threat to Seattle in those harried days of World War II. After all, Japanese forces were known to have reached the Aleutian Islands, which in air miles weren't all that far from the Pacific Northwest. It was believed that wartime Seattle was more likely to experience an attack than any other part of the country. This was based partly on its west coast location, but also because of the defense industries located there—particularly Boeing. Strict blackout requirements were in effect each night, volunteer air wardens were on duty throughout the city, and large buildings kept buckets of sand in the stairwells for possible use in smothering incendiary bombs. Workers flocked to the city to obtain jobs in the war effort. "Rosie the Riveter" became a symbol of the growing number of women on the assembly line.

Boeing operated three shifts every 24 hours to turn out the B-17 Flying Fortresses which played a major role in the eventual winning of the war.

Elliott and I were heading out that morning on a routine test flight on a new B-17. The production flight test people had made a couple of flights to check out everything and make sure it was working properly. When they were satisfied that all was in good order, the airplane was turned over to the experimental flight test department so we could accomplish tests of the new fuel tank vent system which had been installed.

Upon reaching the hangar, we followed our usual practice of boarding the huge plane through the back door, just ahead of the tail. We walked through the rear compartment and headed up the sloping floor toward the nose. The bomb bay was located in the area where the wings join the fuselage. Instead of bombs it housed two ferry tanks of black rubberized fabric. These supplemental fuel tanks would enable it to fly nonstop from the U.S. to England.

The bomb bay catwalk was a narrow bridge about ten inches wide which ran through the center of the fuselage, connecting the rear compartment with the cockpit. About three feet below the catwalk were the closed bomb bay doors which would swing outward to jettison the bombs or fuel tanks.

We picked our way along the catwalk to the cockpit. Elliott's job as pilot in command was to monitor every step of the test to ensure complete accuracy while I flew the plane. Climbing into the copilot's seat, I fastened the safety belt, adjusted my headset, and checked the multitude of gauges, switches and warning lights on the instrument panel. Elliott started the engines, left to right, numbers one, two, three and four.

At the end of the runway I swung the plane into the wind and set the parking brake. Elliott ran up the engines and checked by intercom: "Crew ready for takeoff?" We heard the responses: "Ready up front," and "Ready in the rear." The tower cleared us to roll.

I took off and trimmed the plane to climb west. Below us, the Boeing factory and the airport blended perfectly with the landscape, having been expertly camouflaged to protect them from attack by the Japanese. Burlap buildings and chicken-wire lawns made Plant 2 look like a quiet suburb from the air.

Near Hood Canal I chose an area free of clouds, leveled off at 15,000 feet and prepared for the maximum speed dive which would be a part of our test today. Elliott increased the RPM, advanced the throttles, and adjusted maximum power as I pushed forward on the control wheel and initiated the dive.

Concentrating on the airspeed indicator throughout the dive, I glanced up occasionally to maintain course. As we headed downward I veered to miss a fluffy cumulus cloud, on the chance that it could contain another airplane. When our airspeed reached 300 mph I announced on the intercom, "Speed stabilized—get your data." The flight engineers on board quickly recorded the various system pressures.

Suddenly we experienced a disturbing vibration, but within moments it ceased. Then WHAM! A sudden strong acceleration jammed me down hard into my seat as the plane zoomed sharply upward. I strained to push with both hands on the wheel and with both feet on the column to level the plane, but despite my strenuous efforts the plane continued to climb.

"Help me!" I yelled at Elliott. He too pushed on the controls—to no avail. Neither elevator control nor elevator trim had the slightest effect—we had lost control! The plane seemed to have a mind of its own and continued to shoot skyward for perhaps 1,000 feet. At its apogee, however, it stalled, took a nose dive, and then pulled out, only to zoom upward once again and repeat the frightening dive. With the plane bent on performing aerobatics, there was no chance that we could land it safely. Only one course remained.

Elliott grabbed the microphone and commanded, "Bail out! Bail out!" We had standard procedures for bailing out, but we all still worried about making it out safely.

Ordinarily during the test, flight engineer Ken Luplow would stand just behind our seats. With legs spread for balance, data board in hand, he recorded altitude, airspeed and other readings from the scores of dials on the wide instrument panel. Ken was sharp and accurate, concentrating on his readings during the roughest flights. But now he dropped his data board and grabbed our seat backs to maintain his balance through the first oscillation. Then he made his way with difficulty back to the bomb bay. It was his job to jettison the rubberized fuel tanks so we could bail out through the bomb bay doors.

As copilot, my duty in an emergency would be to hold the plane as steady as possible to let our six-man crew bail out if that became necessary. With the elevator control useless, however, I couldn't control the up and down motion. I could only keep the wings level and fly straight with ailerons and rudder. Soon Elliott yelled "Go on, Marvin, get out." As I stood up, the headset yanked at my ears, and I tore it off. My glasses slid partly off so I tossed them on the floor—they would only break and injure my eyes. As I started toward the bomb bay my chute caught between the seats. I felt a moment of panic, but Elliott twisted the chute so that it would pass through the narrow aisle.

By now the Flying Fortress was giving us a great ride for our money. It stalled again and nosed down, so that I had to raise my arms to keep from bumping my head on the ceiling. Then as the plane recovered from a dive, I was plastered to the deck. When I recovered I groped my way toward the bomb bay, clutching at anything that projected from the wall in order to maintain some semblance of balance.

As I reached the bomb bay I found that Ken was having trouble releasing the fuel tanks. He gave the release handle a strong pull but the tanks failed to jettison. After he kicked them several times they finally released and fell away. As Ken and I stood at the forward end of the open bomb bay, we felt the rush of the airstream and heard the powerful roar of the propellers. The prospect of leaving the plane in this manner was shocking, but we knew that at any moment the plane could plunge downward. Facing us at the rear end of the bomb bay was Cliff Dorman, our 260 lb. radio operator, who had a stunned look on his face. Ken shouted at Cliff to jump, but he seemed undecided. There was no time to lose. I yelled at Cliff "Go ahead and jump!" He disappeared through the open bomb bay doors, and Ken quickly followed.

Now it was my turn. Jumping feet first, I cleared the plane. We were at approximately 10,000 feet when we bailed out, and I felt a blast of very cold air in my face. As I somersaulted downward I saw earth, sky, earth, sky, and knew I mustn't open my chute until I stopped tumbling so the shroud lines wouldn't tangle.

Until now I had no time to be scared. We had rehearsed emergency procedures so often that when the real thing came along I went through the steps automatically. Parachutes are dependable, but there still was doubt in the back of my mind. Shroud lines could tangle and allow the unfortunate victim to fall to earth.

When the tumbling appeared to lessen, I finally gripped the ripcord handle tightly and gave it a healthy pull. Nothing happened. My disoriented view of earth and sky continued for another two seconds, and then the chute popped open with a terrific jolt. I found myself sitting upright in the chute's hammock seat, floating through space while I gave fervent thanks to the Lord that my chute had blossomed.

I felt motionless but knew I was drifting downward. Ever the engineer, I reached for my stop watch to time my descent, but apparently it had snapped off my wrist from the shock of the opening chute. I stuffed the ripcord into a pocket in my flight suit, remembering the parachute jumper's tradition of saving the cord. (I still have it.)

The whole experience seemed unreal as I floated down in the chill air. I could see for miles in all directions. Bremerton, ten miles to the north, seemed close. The snow-capped Olympics stood tall in the west. I was two miles above the earth, suspended motionless in an eerie silence except for the faint sound of the distant airplane. Freed of all human control, the mighty Flying Fortress had the skies to itself. I watched in fascination as it made two wide circles perhaps two miles in diameter, while doing a series of zooms and dives. As the plane gained speed in each dive, I heard the accelerating, angry roar of the propellers. When it slowed down at the top of the zoom, the propellers quieted.

I thought about my wife, Laura, and my two-year old daughter, Carol. What would happen to them if I didn't make it? I worried about the safety of the other crew members. Looking around, I was surprised to see that Ken Luplow was so close I could yell to him.

"Hey Ken, I only see five chutes. How many do you count?"

"Five."

"I wonder if Elliott got out."

At that point the plane circled near enough so that I could see the origin of our problems. Half the tail surface was gone!

"Hey Ken," I yelled, "the left-hand stabilizer and elevator are missing."

"Sure enough. I wonder what happened."

Finally the plane disappeared beneath a cloud and perhaps two minutes later we heard a resounding boom. A huge plume of dense, black smoke rose high in the air from the burning wreckage. There was something at once horrifying and sad about the demise of the Flying Fortress, particularly since we didn't know whether all crew members had survived.

I had a more pressing problem on my mind, however, as I drifted closer to earth. There seemed a distinct possibility that I might land in the chilly waters of Puget Sound, in which case I would either drown or die of hypothermia unless I landed close to the shoreline. At one point I did drift out over the water, but soon drifted back over dry land, and with great relief I noted that my chute and I were headed for a group of tall firs. With a swish the chute deposited me gently on a top limb of a fir, then draped itself over an adjoining tree. I quickly realized that if a gust of wind were to catch the collapsing chute it could drag me from my precarious perch. I had made the 10,000 foot jump safely, only to face the possibility of being killed in a 100 foot fall from a tree.

Until this moment I had been fairly calm and disciplined. I had kept my cool from the time the trouble started—while trying to control the plane, struggling back to the bomb bay and bailing out. But now it was a different matter. The emergency procedures I had followed closely said nothing regarding this situation. Shaking violently, I carefully unfastened the two parachute snaps from the detachable harness with one hand, maintaining a death grip on the tree limb with the other.

Before long I heard shouts, and soon saw four men on the ground below. One man had been working nearby with tree-climbing spikes strapped to his feet. He started up a tree to rescue me, but halfway up he was baffled. "Where are you?" he yelled.

"Here I am," I yelled back, thinking I must be pretty hard to miss.

"Oh hell! I'm in the wrong tree," said my would-be rescuer. He had climbed the neighboring tree containing my chute.

Still shaking, I decided I didn't need a rescuer after all. I asked him to bring down the chute, while I cautiously descended from limb to limb, skinning my knuckles in the process. When I reached the bare trunk I put my arms around it and shinnied the rest of the way down, thanking God that I was at last safely on terra firma.

This appeared to be a bailout that had been carefully choreographed. As if on cue, suddenly three soldiers drove up in their jeep. "We saw you and a couple of other guys coming down in your chutes," one of them said. "Where do you want to go? We'll take you." Gratefully I clambered aboard, carrying my chute.

I mentioned my concern about where the plane had crashed, so the jeep driver followed the column of black smoke to the crash site, which turned out to be a farmer's yard about three miles away. On arrival I was delighted to spot Elliott Merrill approaching.

"Boy, am I glad to see you, Marv!" he said, slapping me heartily on the back.

"Am I glad to see *you*. Ken and I counted only five chutes and wondered if you made it. I see you are limping. Is it bad?"

"Not really," said Elliott. "When I got close to the ground it looked like I was going to fall right into the burning plane, so I steered the chute in a different direction. I ended up drifting backwards through some shrubs, and landed on my back. But considering the alternatives, I think I'm pretty lucky."

Just then Ken appeared, grabbed my hand and pumped it wildly. He had walked barefoot for more than a mile, having lost his loafers mid-air when his chute opened. Elliott, Ken and I were concerned about our other three crew members, Cliff Dorman, Karl Strom and Bob Harlan. We had no idea how to find them. The three of us stood by and watched one area of the scattered wreckage continue to burn furiously. Flames roared skyward, and the heat was so intense we couldn't get close. The smell of gasoline and burning rubber filled the air.

As we poked at the remainder of the wreckage we were joined by the farmer whose yard was the crash scene. "I was sittin' on my porch when I saw that big plane was gonna crash right in my front yard," he said. "The noise of the explosion was terrible. One of those dern engines busted loose and rolled right at me. I took off like a scalded cat!"

One by one, Cliff, Karl and Bob showed up, and we greeted each other with happy shouts and excited hand-shaking. Bob was pretty scratched up.

"I landed in a tree," he explained, "and was hanging in my chute so I couldn't get down. A couple of fellows came and cut the shroud lines to release me." The rescuers saw that Bob was near shock, and gave him a shot of whiskey.

It seemed a miracle that the six of us had escaped with only bruises and scratches. By reason of our jump we had become members of an elite organization—the exclusive Caterpillar Club. Membership is limited to those who bail out of a plane to save their lives. Paratroopers and sky divers are not eligible. A year earlier the famed General Jimmy Doolittle had joined the club by bailing out after his bombing raid over Tokyo. The club got its name because parachutes once were made from silk spun by caterpillars. For some years now I've worn the tiny gold caterpillar insignia in my lapel.

Weeks later the cause of the crash was determined. Careful study revealed that the attachment of the fabric to the elevator framework on the tail had failed. To reduce manhours of construction time, the engineers recently had designed U-shaped clips to fasten the fabric in place. The crash investigation revealed that the clips had failed at the 90-degree bend. As a result of this information, the engineers were able to correct the design before scores of planes were delivered which could have crashed because of this deficiency. Had these planes gone down behind enemy lines, the assumption would have been that they were shot down.

The B-17 already had become the most significant airplane in the European campaign because of its reputation of being almost indestructible. Flying Fortresses had returned safely from combat with half the tail shot away. Unfortunately in our case when half the tail broke away, it tore off the control cables to the remaining half.

Our experience with failure of the U-clips pointed out once again the role of the test pilot and support crew—to locate any weaknesses the plane might have so that they can be corrected before delivery is made and so that appropriate design changes can be accomplished.

Incidentally, a change in dress code for test crews was instituted shortly after our experience. As a result of Ken Luplow's having lost his shoes during the bailout, loafers could no longer be worn on future test flights.

Caterpillar Club members who saved their lives by bailing out. Standing: Marvin Michael, Ken Luplow. Squatting: Cliff Dorman, Bob Harlan, Karl Strom, Elliott Merrill. March 1943

Chapter Eleven

FLYING TOO HIGH WITH SOME GUY IN THE SKY

During my years as a Boeing test pilot I sometimes heard others speak enviously of how wonderful it must be to go on high altitude flight tests and how equally wonderful to draw flight pay. If you will come with me on a typical flight test, I can demonstrate that it wasn't all fun and games.

Jim Fraser, the project pilot on the "Shadow" (the high altitude test B-17 Flying Fortress) is looking for a copilot. He's preparing to run a test at 40,000 feet. "Marv, can you go with us on the Shadow today?"

"Sure," I reply, always eager to be up and away from my desk. (We all spend time wading through the paper work when we aren't assigned to a flight project, and none of us particularly enjoy.) About 9:45 in the morning Jim and I head toward the hangar.

I put on my flying clothes. Because 40,000 feet is considerably higher than we've been going, it is definitely more hazardous. Since this is an unpressurized airplane, Smitty, our training engineer, fixes me up with a special high pressure, high altitude oxygen mask. "How's that? Is it comfortable?"

"Not bad," I reply, although four or five hours of pressure on my face is sure to change my opinion.

Members of the eight-man crew go outside the hangar and connect our masks to 20 foot long rubber hoses radiating from a large oxygen bottle. As we surround the oxygen supply in a circle, we begin a forty-five minute session of breathing pure oxygen. This will remove the nitrogen from our blood and prevent us from getting the bends at high altitude. We toss a ball back and forth so that physical activity will speed up the denitrogenation.

There have been flights where we cut the flight short because a crew member gets the bends. Maybe the oxygen mask is leaking or doesn't fit properly. In such an event it is imperative to land the plane as soon as possible to get treatment for the person in a low pressure chamber. I never had this happen to me, although at times I felt slight symptoms of the bends. I knew a pilot who died because he got the bends.

"How about an electric suit, Marv?" Smitty asks. The electric suit plugs into the airplane electrical system, just like an electric blanket.

I have already dressed rather warmly, but after all, I would rather be too warm than too cold, so I reply, "Bring it on!"

I laboriously remove my outer clothing and don the electric suit. By this time I'm out of breath and in quite a sweat. It's a relief to sit down on the blacktop and fill out the thirty-eight items on the equipment checklist for flights to 40,000 feet or above. We indicate on the list that our oxygen masks fit properly and are functioning correctly.

I check the pressure gauge on my bailout oxygen bottle and securely connect it to my mask. This bottle, the size of a foot-long Polish sausage, fits in a pocket alongside my thigh. In case of an emergency bailout from high altitude, its fifteen-minute oxygen supply will keep me alive until we reach a lower altitude where there is sufficient oxygen in the atmosphere to sustain life.

With two-gallon oxygen bottles slung over our shoulders, we trudge out to the Shadow, check out the engines, and take off. I do the flying because as project pilot, Jim's responsibility is to carefully monitor the test to make sure everything is accomplished according to a precise schedule.

During the climb I become painfully aware of the pressure from a part of the mask I call the crupper, a rubber strap which goes under my nose just like the crupper on a set of harness goes under the horse's tail. Boeing Radio calls to warn us that the weather bureau is predicting the weather over Seattle will close in sooner than predicted in an earlier forecast. They promise to keep us alerted, but we make a mental note to check back with them. They sometimes forget to update the weather predictions for us.

As we continue our climb I feel my headset tugging, so I lean forward to untangle the cord. As I bend over, the moisture which has condensed inside my mask trickles down my chin, and soon my nose begins to drip as well. It itches in the worst way; however I am powerless to relieve the itching. I screw up my face and endure it. Presently my eyes begin to water, perhaps in sympathy for my nose.

Now a blast of cold air strikes my leg, yet elsewhere I am sweating profusely. I look around in vain for a parachute bag or something to cover my leg. I shrug my shoulders and give up.

As we climb above the clouds I am nearly blinded by the glare of the sun, so I reach for my sunglasses. I then recall that this is a 40,000 foot mask with helmet and appendages and it would be too difficult to fit my glasses in and around the helmet and mask. I squint and endure it.

We've been flying at 120 miles per hour; we are now at 39,000 feet and our rate of climb has dropped to almost zero. Jim says, "Let's try zooming—see if we can get up a little higher." It's almost like lifting ourselves by our bootstraps, for now we must slowly and gingerly lose a little altitude in order to gain additional speed. We don't dare lose altitude too fast or we will lose everything we expect to gain by the zooming maneuver. With the additional speed attained, I gently ease back on the control wheel to gain altitude. Rough handling of the controls would increase drag and keep the plane from reaching maximum performance.

The zooming maneuver works! At 40,000 we level off and gradually, by handling the controls very delicately, we get up to 145 mph. As our airspeed picks up, the right wing becomes heavy. The aileron trim tab would remove the heaviness, but I have no trim control at my station.

I start to ask Jim to adjust the trim control at his station. But the pressure to my oxygen mask has now been turned up so high that it is extremely difficult to talk. I simply give up, concluding it is easier to fight the controls than to make Jim understand.

The oxygen pressure is so great that it fills my lungs almost instantaneously, and I must make a great effort to exhale. In the normal breathing process, inhaling requires effort and exhaling is effortless. But when wearing the pressure mask, if I should force air out too fast by exhaling, my lungs will immediately fill up with oxygen and I will have the exhaling effort to go through again. Then I will be panting—breathing two or three times as fast as I should. If hyperventilation continues for only a few minutes, dizziness will result and then coma. I must, therefore, concentrate on keeping my breathing normal, just to stay alive.

The pressure of the helmet and headset on my ears has become almost unbearable. Also, with the oxygen pressure turned up high, crew members' voices over the interphone are so muffled I have to press the headset tightly against my ears with both hands to understand them. Since I must hold the airplane's altitude precisely, I can't release the controls to grip the earphones every time I want to hear someone talk. I remove the headset to relieve the pressure on my ears.

The continuous deafening roar of the four engines and the vibration almost set my teeth to chattering. The sun beating in through the window makes me warm, and I am becoming very drowsy. It's so restful to close my eyes for a moment or two, but I struggle to force them open to make sure we are holding our precise altitude.

If only I could break out my thermos for a cup of coffee! No, that wouldn't work; we couldn't drink coffee at 40,000 feet with these masks.

As I turn toward Jim, my oxygen mask hose gives a tug. Looking down, I note that the oxygen mask hose, bailout bottle hose, headset cord, microphone cord, electric suit cord, parachute harness, safety belt and life vest all are tangled and caught on the seat adjustment handle. With one hand on the controls, I attempt with the other to unscramble the mess.

Time is passing very slowly now. If only I could stand up and stretch. I'm so sore I swear I'll never sit down again for days. In the cramped cockpit I can't squirm around enough to get into a more comfortable position. At last I ask Jim in sign language if he will fly the ship for a few minutes while I rest, and he agrees. Efforts to massage my aching ears through the thickness of the helmet are futile. I close my eyes and try to relax for a few moments, but pains, brought on by the beginning symptoms of the bends, torture my body so that I'm obsessed with my misery.

Hunger pangs are gnawing. It was nearly lunchtime when we completed our preflight denitrogenation back at the hangar, but we couldn't stop to eat then. We took off at noon, and it is now 3:30 p.m. with the end of the flight still not in sight. I have a candy bar in my briefcase, but I would have to make a great effort to request over the interphone that Kenny, the flight engineer, hand it to me, as I'm too hemmed in to reach it. Oh well, I couldn't eat anything now if I *could* get hold of it. While one might lift the oxygen mask sufficiently to eat a few bites at 25,000 feet, to do so at 40,000 feet would be suicide. Just a slight loss of oxygen pressure at this altitude and you would be unconscious in 20 to 30 seconds. My mouth waters as I think of that luscious candy bar.

Jim raises his hands, flashes ten fingers at me twice, and then points down. Ah! What a relief to know that in

20 minutes we will start our descent. After another 18 agonizing minutes elapse, Jim calls over the interphone that perhaps we should stay here an additional 15 minutes. I am bitterly disappointed, although I realize that another quarter hour of data-gathering, now that we're up here may save hours of climbing in the future. It helps somewhat to know that the rest of the crew is as uncomfortable as I am.

Nevertheless, in my groggy condition it seems the world is cruel to force me to endure 15 minutes more of torture.

After a painful eternity Jim points downward and we begin the descent. You would think we could just chop the throttles and be on the ground in a few minutes. No way. In a high speed descent the engine cylinder heads would suffer thermal shock from the rush of cold air; the sudden cooling would crack them and the engines would fail.

Besides, our ears would plug up if we came down too fast. (Airline passengers today aren't bothered unless they have a bad cold. With a pressurized cabin, they never get above 10,000 feet cabin altitude.)

Now that we're down to a relatively safe 25,000 feet, I look forward to a cup of steaming coffee from my thermos. As I unscrew the stopper, suddenly a fountain of hot coffee explodes and sprays the ceiling. To my great disappointment, only a few drops remain in the thermos. I hadn't realized that with the low atmospheric pressure at 25,000 feet the hot coffee would be way above boiling point. When I removed the stopper the coffee boiled instantly and erupted like Old Faithful.

When we reach 5,000 feet in our descent, it begins to rain in the cockpit. The exploding coffee had frozen on the uninsulated subzero ceiling. Now that the plane has warmed up at the lower altitude, the melting coffee is raining on us.

Well, another day in the life of a test pilot. While flying at 40,000 feet isn't all that much fun, the test we conducted today is important, and I know that if Jim asks me again tomorrow I'll go. I don't have to enjoy it. The knowledge of a job to be done outweighs the discomfort, and any real achievement requires sacrifice. Flight pay is great, but the real payoff on this job is the satisfaction of having added to the world's body of scientific knowledge by pioneering in flight research.

Test pilot Marvin Michael at controls of Boeing B-29 Superfortress bomber. 1944

Chapter Twelve

THE SUPERFORTRESS:
A QUANTUM LEAP

The B-29 Superfortress, silhouetted against the early morning sky at the Smoky Hill Army Air Field in Salina, Kansas, that September day of 1944, excited me. Although I had flown B-29's before, they still seemed huge compared to the B-17 Flying Fortress. As I walked under the wings spanning 141 feet, the long fuselage stretched out before me, loaded to the design capacity with 10,000 pounds of sand-filled dummy bombs and 7,329 gallons of fuel.

The Superfortress took a quantum leap in new technologies never before tested in flight. Its load capacity per square foot of wing area was substantially higher than on any previous plane. Designed to accomplish distant bombing missions, the B-29 offered unprecedented long-range capability. It contained innovations such as a pressurized cabin and tricycle landing gear, comprised of two nose wheels, two left main wheels, and two right main wheels.

My assignment was to fly a sustained 3,200 miles without landing, in order to test the B-29's ability to perform long-range bombing missions. As I climbed the ladder to the entry hatch, I felt a thrill of anticipation for this challenging mission. I was joined in the cockpit by my copilot, John Fornasero, who was a few years my senior (I was 32). He was short and dapper, with brown eyes and a thin black mustache. We both were aware that there could be no mistakes in testing this Boeing giant. The war was going poorly for our troops in the Pacific. Success in these tests would mean a tremendous advantage over our enemies, and could shorten the war. The Air Force was pressuring Boeing for immediate results.

With our crew of eight aboard, I checked the many instruments on the panel and instructed the flight engineer to start the engines. We were ready to taxi out for our before-takeoff checklist runup.

"Tower gave us runway two five," said John.

"Check crew ready for takeoff," I replied. "Remind them to stand by in case we have to abort." We all knew this was a high risk takeoff, since the B-29 had not yet been tested for the capacity load of bombs and fuel which we were carrying. The crew needed to be ready to exit the plane in a hurry if things went wrong.

My right hand gripped the wheel as I opened the throttles with my left hand until the engines were at full power, then released the brakes. The big plane moved slowly down the runway and then picked up speed. As we accelerated, Fornasero called out our speeds: "100...110...120...130..." I pulled back on the wheel and felt the plane airborne, but it seemed reluctant to climb. I held my breath. We stayed low until the airspeed built up. A minute after takeoff, the right hand engine observer yelled on intercom, "Number three engine is covered with oil!" My stomach flipped.

I couldn't see the engine, but number three oil pressure gauge read zero. In a matter of seconds the engine would freeze up and fail. Quickly I feathered the propeller to reduce the drag and stop the engine. I hit the emergency bomb jettison control and released the 10,000 pounds of dummy bombs in hopes the other three engines would keep us airborne. The plane wasn't designed to dump fuel or that would have gone too.

I clung to the wheel with sweaty palms as the huge plane staggered to an altitude of 500 feet. I gently banked and turned left. Fornasero radioed the tower, "Air Force 528, we lost an engine. Request emergency clearance to land."

With the three remaining experimental engines forced to pull emergency power, I knew that one or more of them could fail at any moment. Nevertheless, I flew a wide traffic pattern to permit a careful rundown of the landing checklist, with an airspeed of 170 miles per hour. Although dropping the bombs had given us a better landing gross weight, the heavy load of fuel meant that this had to be a "greased on" landing. I had to make a perfectly smooth touchdown or risk collapsing the landing gear.

Nobody wanted to survive this flight more than I did. That big bird touched down at the beginning of the runway with a CRUMPH! We decelerated and came to a stop close to the end of the runway. Neither Fornasero nor I could move. He looked over at me, grinned, and gave me a thumbs-up. Grim and shaking, I said, "I hope we have better luck on the next try!"

We learned the bombs landed harmlessly in a farmer's field.

Mechanics worked around the clock for two days to repair the broken oil line. The fuel tanks were topped off, a new 5-ton load of sand bombs placed aboard, and once more we were ready for takeoff. Safely airborne without incident, we cruised northeastward at 235 miles per hour. We passed over Chicago and headed southeast. Over Washington, D.C. we turned south toward the Myrtle Beach bombing range off the coast of South Carolina. Over the intercom I called Bob Britton, the bombardier-engineer. "Stand by, Bob. We're approaching the test target at 29,000 feet, per flight plan."

At this point I gave control of the plane to the bombardier. Bob guided the plane over the target by autopilot and announced, "Bombs away."

The right engine observer yelled on intercom, "Five bombs failed to release."

I banked the plane to make another run and ordered, "All crew members don oxygen masks. We're depressurizing to release bombs manually."

Once more Britton guided the plane over the target. Using portable oxygen, the right hand observer entered the bomb bay, jiggled the bomb release and the bombs fell free. "Marv, bombs released," he said. "It's all yours."

I again took control of the plane and we headed west. With our bombs delivered I had a pleasant feeling of accomplishment, which didn't last long. As we approached Marietta, Georgia, Fornasero fiddled with the autopilot. He turned to me with a scowl and said, "Marv, I can't get this darn thing to work."

"Well," I said, "Good thing we know how to fly it manually."

Heading southwest toward New Orleans, three fourths of the way through our scheduled flight time, we encountered a violent thunderstorm. Severe static garbled our radio reception, making it impossible to hear the weather reports.

"Looks pretty bad," said Fornasero.

"What do you think, John—shall we try to fly around it?"

"It's worth a try," he replied.

John had done more instrument flying than I, and I valued his expertise. The storm turned out to be too widespread to fly around it. We would have had to go too far out of our way. We then attempted to fly directly through the storm, heading toward Wichita. The air became extremely turbulent and the plane bounced so much that we couldn't read the instruments on the panel. After about ten minutes of bucking the storm we gave up and abandoned the plan. We knew our fuel must be running low, but because the buffeting of the storm prevented our reading the gauges we couldn't tell exactly how much was left. Fearing that we couldn't make it to Wichita, we turned around and headed for Fort Worth, Texas.

We were out of the storm, but not yet out of the woods. The left hand observer came on the intercom: "Marv, I think you ought to know that number one engine has been letting a few sparks go every once in a while."

"Thanks. Instruments look OK. Keep a sharp eye and let me know if it gets worse."

Fatigued from stress, we were tense with apprehension as we prepared to land at a strange field after dark, but the landing at 9:17 p.m. was uneventful. We experienced a great sense of relief as we taxied in and parked.

A very tired and stiff flight crew staggered out of the airplane. We had been airborne for 13 hours and 40 minutes. We stretched our aching limbs as we walked up and down waiting for taxis. It took us two days to rest up in our hotel while mechanics prepared the plane for our return trip.

As we re-entered the airport we saw dozens of people peering through the fence for a glimpse of the Superfortress. As we walked onto the field I'm sure other crew members shared my feeling of pride that we were associated with this shining new superplane. When we were preparing to board the plane for the final leg, the mechanic reported, "Marv, we found the sparks were caused by a broken exhaust pipe. We were able to weld it up in good shape."

I was greatly relieved that the trouble had been found, realizing we were fortunate that the sparks hadn't set the plane on fire. We had long ago accepted the fact that this was an experimental flight test, and malfunctions were to be expected. Repairs and servicing accomplished, we returned the plane to home base. We had completed the 3,200 miles but because of the malfunctions and poor weather, Boeing engineers scheduled a repeat flight.

* * * *

The second flight, made in December, presented its own set of difficulties. Because the days were shorter it would be impossible to complete the entire flight in daylight. It is highly desirable to accomplish such test flights in daylight because accuracy is greater and it is easier for the crew to record data.

Senior Flight Test Engineer Bob Britton was exceptionally talented. He was the genius who supervised much of the operational planning of the flight. Bob and I discussed flight plans. Should we take off in daytime and land after dark, or vice versa?

Bob said, "Since a maximum gross weight takeoff is the most dangerous part of the flight, shouldn't we take off in daylight so the engine observers in the rear will have a clear view of the engines?"

"Good point," I acknowledged. '"On the other hand, it's important that we locate our destination and make the landing in daylight, since we'll be dead tired after 13 hours of flying."

In the end an ingenious installation of landing lights was made which would illuminate the engines at night, and the takeoff was made in the early morning darkness. In order to get two additional hours of daylight, we decided to take off again from Salina, Kansas, and follow the sun around to Seattle.

The selection of food for a 13-hour flight was crucial. If the food was not appetizing and did not supply sufficient energy, crew members could not perform their tasks efficiently and accurately. We took sandwiches, soup, beverages, fruit and pastries. The crew expressed a liking for cream of tomato soup. I wished to allow no small detail to detract from the success of the flight, so I carried a half dozen cans of tomato soup in my suitcase from Seattle to Salina, to make sure crew members would have their preference.

Our plan was to fly southwest across Oklahoma and Texas, then head west to drop our bombs in the ocean off the coast of California. The evening before our scheduled takeoff the forecast called for heavy fog along the west coast, from Canada to Mexico. Radar bombing would have enabled us to locate our ocean bombing range through the fog, but unfortunately it was not available to us. Because of the fog we had to switch to a smaller, land-based target, which required more precision bombing. This could be accomplished only with a new instrument, the top secret Norden bombsight.

The new Norden bombsight was coupled to the autopilot and represented the most advanced technology. It was used in nearly all bombing operations by the United States in World War II, and was largely responsible for the U.S. Air Force success in bombing Germany. The bombardier guarded it with his life.

Bob Britton hastily took a short briefing on operation of the bombsight at the Bombardier's School at the Salina Air Field. Armed with a six-page abbreviated set of instructions, Bob boarded the plane with the rest of the crew for a 5:43 a.m. takeoff.

In order to accomplish the required 3,200 air miles, we flew a circuitous route which took us over Oklahoma City, El Paso, back over Oklahoma City, then Kansas City and out to the bombing range a hundred miles west of Kansas City. While flying this course we needed to radio the appropriate Air Force official for permission to use the bombing range. We had to wait until their office hours opened, with further valuable time required to locate the proper officer. This delay, combined with annoying radio static and the need to maintain precision navigation, made for a very frustrating experience, but finally we arrived at the target area.

Because the automatic pilot failed most of the time on this flight, I had to fly the airplane manually over the target through instructions from the bombardier.

Ordinarily he would have flown the plane through use of the automatic pilot. After guiding me over the target Bob yelled, "Bombs away!"

The right engine observer called on intercom, "Nine bombs failed to release."

I was able to drop seven of them with the emergency release control, but we had to carry the last two home in the plane. Although this offered no serious problem for us, on a combat mission it would present a hazard to land with bombs still aboard. Our experience in this regard would no doubt send the engineers back to the drawing board. This was just one example of the valuable data gained from our test flights.

We all breathed easier after our bombs had reached their target. We then flew over North Platte, Nebraska; Cheyenne and Rock Springs, Wyoming, and Pocatello, Idaho. An earlier weather forecast had called for only scattered clouds from Cheyenne to Seattle, but an update had my copilot obviously concerned as he advised me "Marv, the entire Pacific Coast west of Salt Lake City, from Canada to Mexico, is covered with low stratus clouds, below minimums for landing."

We feverishly calculated a revised route and a final destination in order to complete the desired mileage and still land at a base able to service a B-29. We chose Billings, Montana, as our destination. My eyes were tired and my back ached from sitting still so many hours as we flew north toward Butte and then east to Billings, where we made an uneventful landing.

On this flight, the automatic pilot had worked only three of the 13 hours and 25 minutes we were in the air. The autopilot malfunction and poor weather kept me so busy that I never once left my seat for the entire period. I was so stiff I could barely stumble out of the plane.

Once we had landed at Billings, here too, crowds of civilians gathered for a glimpse from a distance of the Superfortress. With the top secret Norden bombsight aboard, we had to provide security by hiring armed guards around the clock until we departed Billings.

With the completion of these two lengthy flight tests of the B-29 Superfortress, my crew and I felt a great sense of accomplishment. It was yet another demonstration of the grand struggle against big odds toward an achievement—in this case, the collection of vital B-29 operational data. This in turn enabled Air Force crews to fly the B-29 so efficiently that the war ended substantially sooner. It took our crew three days to rest up and recover from the ordeal.

Boeing B-29 Superfortress flown in flight research for
three years by Marvin Michael and crew. 1949

Marvin Michael, in Boeing B-50 Superfortress receiver
(below) refuels from Boeing B-29 tanker (above). 1950

Chapter Thirteen

LOWERING THE BOOM

The year was 1949. It had been four years since the end of World War II but the cold war still held world powers in its grip, and defense spending remained a major item in our national budget. Although Boeing was placing increased emphasis on providing the world with the latest and best in transcontinental airliners, it maintained its efforts to supply the military with valuable technological improvements. Test pilots continued to play an important role in these efforts.

The concept of aerial refueling, initiated by the British, became an important adjunct in our national security program, since it could bring the most remote targets within the bombsights of American planes. The technology of the available refueling process left a lot to be desired, however, both with regard to safety and in terms of results achieved. At the request of Air Force officials, Boeing sought a method of refueling in the air that was more reliable and efficient than the cumbersome British hose method being tested.

Thus it was that Project Engineer Cliff Leisy and I were sent to Wichita to observe the British hose system of refueling and initiate a study of what could be done to improve upon it. We watched the operation from the air and saw that it was very hazardous and awkward, involving difficult flying maneuvers.

The crew of the tanker plane would release one end of a length of hose, and the pilot of the receiver plane would attempt to make a lateral pass with a grappling hook to snag it. Under the best of conditions it was difficult to catch the trailing hose, and the rate of fuel transfer was limited. In turbulent conditions the British system was totally unworkable. It was unsatisfactory to the Air Force, who wanted something faster and more dependable.

Back in Seattle after the demonstration, Cliff and I agreed that our first task was to determine the most favorable position for the receiver and the tanker during fuel transfer. We took off in two B-29 Superfortresses, with one crew flying the simulated tanker. Cliff rode with me in the simulated receiver, as we tried all refueling positions imaginable. I flew above, below and out to the side of the tanker while we evaluated the efficiency of each position.

"Cliff," I told him, "I think the optimum position for the receiver is about 10 feet behind and 25 feet below the tanker; that provides the best visibility for the receiver pilot."

He agreed, then described his idea for attaching a rigid boom to the tail end of the tanker. He and his engineering group designed a boom consisting of two telescoping sections of pipe with a "butterfly" tail surface. The tail had two short stubby wings in a V-configuration which allowed the boom operator to actually "fly" that length of pipe with a conventional airplane-type control stick. The airstream acted upon the two control surfaces—the "ruddevators"—providing the force needed to raise, lower, or swing the boom. Guiding this innovative contraption called for excellent coordination and a pretty good knowledge of piloting.

In our initial tests the boom operator was a fellow named Bert Binegar, a flight test engineer in his early 30's who wore thick glasses and spoke with a slow drawl. To operate the boom he stretched out face down on a special pallet in the tail of the tanker. His head was toward the rear of the plane, and he was able to look down and back through a view window.

Our first tests, of course, weren't to transfer fuel, but to check the mating compatibility of the receiver and the tanker. From his spread eagle position Bert "flew" the boom, moving it up and down, side to side, and running it through various test conditions.

Back on the ground, adjustments were made based on the results of our efforts. The ruddevators were again flight tested, and we were ready for the next phase—in-flight mating.

I took to the air in the B-29 receiver, which was fitted with a dummy receptacle on top of the plane, above the aft end of the cockpit compartment. As I approached the tanker I radioed Bert that I was a half-mile behind and closing. I then slowed down and closed in cautiously, being careful not to overrun the tanker. In aiming for the receiver position we had established as optimum, I was well aware of the inherent hazard in maneuvering two large airplanes in such proximity. The danger of colliding with the tanker was very real and frightening.

As we got close, the receiver plane began to shift slowly from side to side despite my efforts to control it. I couldn't seem to make it hover directly behind the tanker. I felt humiliated. There was my flight crew watching, and I was unable to make the plane do what it was supposed to do. With practice, however, I learned that I was overcontrolling by using the ailerons—the control surfaces out on the wings which caused the plane to turn right or left. I had to curb my instinct to use the ailerons and instead learned to control the sideways movement with swift, hard jabs on the rudder pedals. This was probably the first tight formation flying performed with such large airplanes.

As I finally stabilized the receiver plane close to the refueling position, Bert directed me: "Up two feet and forward four feet." When I reached the proper position Bert lowered the boom, pointed it toward the receptacle, and extended the inside pipe hydraulically. With practice he was able to make the end of the boom lightly touch the receptacle on the receiver plane. We had passed the first hurdle.

The next step was to equip the tanker plane with a complete fuel transfer system. Having proved the mating maneuver with boom and receiver was feasible, we now had to demonstrate pumping practicability, and we did this first with water. We were elated that the system worked.

The final step would be an actual fuel transfer, a process fraught with worries. When we made the water transfer there had been a significant amount of spillage. Our concern now was that the fuel spillage might be even greater. We were concerned that a spark of static electricity could ignite the fuel and blow us right out of the sky, so we approached the transfer very, very cautiously.

On a gray November morning we took off from Boeing Field—the tanker crew first, followed by my crew in the receiver. My concentration for this final test wasn't helped by the presence of a C-97 Stratofreighter filled with Air Force generals and Boeing company officials, who were observing the entire procedure from just off my right wing.

We climbed to 7,000 feet, and I started closing in on the tanker. I tried to ignore the numerous pairs of eyes staring at us from the C-97.

"Are you about ready to make contact, Marv?" Bert Binegar asked me. "Roger," I told him. He began to direct me, and I crept closer.

"Come forward five feet, Marv. Forward four...three...two..." he refined it down until I was in the refueling position. There was just enough air turbulence to make it difficult to stay in the nominal contact position. Sweat crept down my forehead, and I couldn't wipe it off.

I heard a "CRUMPH!" above and behind me. "Contact made," came Bert's voice. Then: "You're over-running a little, Marv." He corrected my position—pulled me back two feet. Then I heard his voice again: "Fuel pump on." My hands were sweaty, and it was hard to keep a tight grip on the wheel and throttles.

A few seconds later I heard Bert again. This time he was elated: "Fuel flow 200 gallons per minute!"

I knew we had done it, but I couldn't relax just yet. The possibility of a fuel explosion on disconnect was very much on my mind. Besides, we didn't need to transfer a lot of fuel.

"That's enough, Bert," I told him, "go ahead and disconnect.'" The boom retracted, and I reduced throttle and backed off. No explosion, but a big sigh of relief.

Immediately from the C-97 we heard the voice of General George Mundy, with the Air Materiel Command: "Congratulations! Good job!"

We took a deep breath and headed for home, exhausted but exhilarated.

This successful effort did not mean the end of our research and development work to refine the boom operation. In subsequent tests I sometimes flew the receiver plane, and at other times flew the tanker. My copilot on an extended series of flights with the tanker plane was a fellow named Dave. He had never checked out as first pilot, so he always flew as copilot. One of the most interesting and challenging parts of any flight is the landing; usually the opportunity to land the plane alternated between pilot and copilot. On three flights in a row, however, there had been stiff crosswinds and other complications so I had landed the plane rather than letting Dave bring it in.

On the next flight out I decided to give Dave his turn at landing the plane. In these refueling test flights we were constantly aware that gasoline is a very volatile substance, and that we needed to treat it with great respect. On this particular flight we smelled gas fumes in the bomb bay. Realizing that a spark from the electric motor operating the wing flaps could trigger an explosion, I told Dave we'd better not use the wing flaps on landing. That meant our approach and landing speeds would be higher than normal.

"Boeing Radio, this is Air Force 921," I radioed. "We have gas fumes in the bomb bay, so we're landing flaps up." I then said to Dave, "Maintain 20 mph higher speed on approach and landing."

Everything looked good until we were ten feet above the runway, when Dave suddenly closed the throttles. BONG! We hit the ground with such force we were nearly jolted out of our seats. The closing of the throttles instantly produced so much drag from the four 16-foot diameter propellers that we had literally stalled the airplane. A loud clatter broke out in the rear.

"The boom broke away from the tail and it's dragging!" the boom operator yelled in alarm.

Had we been flying a more vulnerable type of airplane than the hefty Superfortress, Dave's landing could easily have destroyed the landing gear.

After the flight, Dave explained his rationale for having closed the throttles. He had been afraid the 20 additional miles per hour might make us run off the far end of the 10,000 foot runway (an extremely remote possibility). Once he closed the throttles, no one could have opened them fast enough to prevent the stall. Yet as pilot-in-command I knew I would bear the responsibility for the accident. My face flushed and I had a sensation of near-panic with the realization of what this could do to my career.

Two days later the data analysts presented me with a plot of the airspeed and altitude throughout the landing. Each plane we tested was equipped with a photorecorder camera, which took a series of photos of the special instrument panel throughout the flight. Fortunately the camera for this trip got the whole story, second by second. It clearly showed the landing approach was right on until Dave chopped the throttles. No pilot-in-command could have prevented the accident once the throttles were closed.

I was exonerated, but I felt bad about the cost and delay to the test program. The accident report undoubtedly found its way into Dave's company file, but he was allowed to continue with Boeing as a copilot, although he never did check out as first pilot. He probably had an interesting story to tell his grandchildren, if he was willing to admit it.

I trained and checked out other Boeing test pilots on receiver pilot technique. I found that even our most experienced pilots had difficulty overcoming their instinct to control the plane's sideways movement by using the ailerons, but eventually they mastered the technique of applying sharp jabs of the rudder pedals to stop the sashaying.

Later Boeing sent me to Air Force bases around the country to teach tanker and receiver pilot techniques. That year I was out of town four months on Boeing assignments, and I was rather unhappy about that. Even unhappier was Laura, my wife, who had three small children to care for and a household to maintain, with an absentee husband. I felt I could not jeopardize my job by refusing the assignments, however.

In May, 1950, the Air Force asked Boeing to put on an in-flight refueling demonstration at Wright Patterson Air Force Base in Dayton, Ohio, as a part of the Air Force Day celebration. Captain Zack Gray, a pilot who was on the Air Force plant staff at Boeing, flew a B-29 tanker and I flew a B-50 receiver to Dayton.

The B-50 was a greatly improved B-29. It flew faster, had a boosted (powered) rudder, a steerable nose wheel, electric rather than hydraulically controlled propellers, and other improvements.

The Air Force asked us to demonstrate in-flight refueling at 1,500 feet above the ground so the big-wigs could see it better. We had never done it at this low an altitude and I was disturbed at the prospect, but it was their show. The day was very hot and the B-50 had no air conditioning. I sweated profusely, both from the heat and the stress. The air was extremely turbulent, adding to the difficulty of hooking up with the tanker. Bert Binegar was operating the boom in Zack's B-29, and despite my concerns about the altitude all went well. Bert cued me into position, made the contact, and we held it until out of sight of the VIP's, then broke off and returned to the field.

For the return flight to Seattle, Zack pulled rank on me. "I need to get back to the office quicker," he said. "I'll take the B-50 and you can return the B-29 to Seattle." My crew and I weren't too happy about getting stuck with the B-29.

We took off for Seattle with plenty of fuel. After a few hours I noticed the autopilot wouldn't maintain level flight, but kept gaining and losing altitude. Over South Dakota our flight engineer, Aubrey Leonard, called on intercom, "I don't understand it, Marv. We're using more fuel than we should."

"Do you have any clue as to what could be causing it?" I asked.

"No...everything else looks normal."

I considered the possibility of a fuel leak. "Blister observers," I called, "Have you seen any evidence of fuel leaking?"

"No, none at all," they replied.

"All crew members: Keep a sharp eye on everything and keep me informed of anything suspicious," I requested.

The autopilot gradually got worse. It was cranking in more nose-down trim, but I couldn't see how that would have anything to do with our excessive fuel consumption. I was getting more frustrated and worried by the minute.

Over Montana, Aubrey said, "Marv, at this rate I calculate we'll run out of fuel before we reach Seattle. What do you want to do?"

I checked the map for some place where we could refuel an Air Force plane. "Just to be on the safe side," I said, "I think we'd better land at the Great Falls Air Force Base and take on more fuel."

Upon reaching Great Falls I brought the plane in with an uneventful landing approach. As we slowed down on the landing rollout I noticed that the nose of the plane bobbed up and down. Very strange! Even though I applied the brakes gently, down went the nose. As we parked, a couple of the fellows in the cockpit opened the hatch and dropped to the ground. Immediately the nose started to go up!

I yelled at them, "Jump back in here *quick*, and you fellows in the back end, come forward *pronto!*" For some unknown reason the Superfortress wanted to sit back on its tail. We radioed for a fuel truck, then started looking for the trouble. We soon located the problem. The valve between the forward and rear bomb bay tanks had remained open, when it should have been closed. Fuel had flowed by gravity from the forward to the rear tank, moving our center of gravity way back. No wonder the autopilot malfunctioned and the plane wanted to sit on its tail. This was an extremely unstable and dangerous situation. We had come very close to losing control and crashing.

When the fuel truck arrived I said to the driver, "I'm embarrassed to tell you we don't need gas. But could you pump gas from our rear bomb bay tank into our front tank?" That being done, we took off and the remainder of our flight to Seattle was uneventful.

****

The work we accomplished had far-reaching ramifications in the annals of military aviation. Although the technology of in-flight refueling has been greatly refined since our work in 1949, the basic procedures we developed have continued to benefit military aviation throughout the world. The procedure is not used for civilian aviation because it is considered somewhat dangerous. The danger is acceptable for the military. Not every military flight is equipped for it, but many are. In the Persian Gulf war, in-flight refueling was critical.

I look back on my role as project test pilot in the development of in-flight refueling procedures as one of my most interesting and challenging assignments at Boeing.

Boeing KC-97 Tanker. 1952

Chapter Fourteen

IS THIS ALL THERE IS?

By age 39 I'd had all sorts of wonderful aviation adventures. I had soared with sailplane wings like an eagle; achieved my boyhood dream of flying huge airplanes worldwide; published many articles in magazines. I'd fallen in love and married a wonderfully charming and talented woman; taken my children camping and engaged in Scouting activities with them.

People would say to me, "You must be one of the happiest people on earth!"

But I wasn't. Something was wrong, and I didn't know what. I was frequently worried, and bitter over trivial things. I wanted my own airplane more than anything in the world. I'd achieved recognition as a Boeing test pilot and was well paid, but the children's education and other expenses mounted. I felt utterly frustrated. A dear friend suggested that life might be more enjoyable if I just gave up the idea of ever having my personal plane. Unthinkable!

Worry was ever present. Depression plagued me. We spent too much money on music lessons for Carol, Gwen, Mike and Larry. I wasn't able to buy the dream house that Laura wanted. Our friends took exotic vacations which we couldn't afford.

Night after night, when sleep eluded me, I stumbled out of bed and read until I grew weary enough to collapse. My doctor gave me sleeping pills, which upset Laura and precipitated many arguments. When I had trouble staying awake at work, usually in the middle of the afternoon, the doctor gave me Dexedrine to keep me awake. I was popping uppers and downers long before it became the "in" thing to do. Years later I learned that the Dexedrine most likely contributed heavily to my constant irritability.

What was wrong? We went to church every Sunday and took the children to Sunday School. When I occasionally tried to read the Bible, it was too hard to understand. My perfunctory prayers changed nothing. I didn't drink, smoke, swear, or tell dirty stories. But I was very unhappy. I knew something was wrong, but my struggles to find the cause were fruitless.

At about this time some close friends invited Laura and me to a couples conference at The Firs—a Bible conference ground 90 miles north of Seattle. The cabins, dormitory, dining and meeting rooms were nestled among tall fir trees. People went there from all over the Northwest for weekend or week-long conferences. The food and fellowship were enjoyable. We began attending two or three conferences a year, where we listened to some of the best Bible teachers in the world. The Bible increasingly came alive.

But what I heard there started to bother me. Other conferees seemed happy. I sensed their joy and their commitment to God, and it made me uncomfortable. My uneasy feeling came with the realization that compared to these teachers and conferees, I had just been *playing* church.

One conference we attended was especially unsettling. I woke up about four o'clock one morning and couldn't go back to sleep. Laura was sleeping soundly. Carefully climbing out of bed, I slipped on my shirt, slacks and shoes. Tiptoeing out of the bedroom, I strolled pensively in the early morning light beneath the majestic trees. My steps sank deep into the cushion of fir needles. I breathed in the heavenly fragrance of the woods, which were perfectly still except for the occasional twitter of a bird. The words of the Bible teachers ran through my mind. "Come to me all you who labor and are heavy laden and I will give you rest." But I wasn't experiencing rest or peace.

Suddenly it came to me. If God exists—if he is REAL—then my relationship to him is THE MOST IMPORTANT THING IN THE WORLD. And if my relationship is right, then nothing else really matters! Yet I struggled with the implications. If I followed my overwhelming impulse to turn my life over to God would I need to give up my dream of having my plane? Having fun?

Finally I said, "Lord, you take my life and run it—I can't. I've been trying to live my life in my own strength. I need your strength." With some hesitation I added, "And Lord, if you want me to have my own airplane, that would be wonderful—but if you don't want me to have it, that's all right too!" At that very instant I felt as if a ton of lead was lifted abruptly from my shoulders. Tears of joy trickled down my face. My commitment to total obedience to God and His Word, the Bible, became the turning point in my life. It became clear to me that until now my work, not God, had been my lord.

The daily battle did not evaporate. Of course I would stumble, but God's forgiveness was always there. From that moment on, however, I no longer needed sleeping and wakeup pills. To be sure I still wanted very much to have my own airplane, but I knew I could be content without it, resting securely in the thought that if it was God's will, in his own good time I would have it.

Truthfully I can say I have never worried since that moment. For me, worry is undue care and anxiety, bordering on despair. I've felt concern as to how the children were doing in school or how we'd pay the bills at the end of the month, but I've never really worried. There's no need to, for the Bible says, "My God will supply all your needs according to His riches in Christ Jesus."[1] He didn't say He would supply all my wants and desires, but He did promise to supply all of my *needs*. Still, the daily struggle remains. Indeed, the Bible says that all who desire to live godly lives will be persecuted. But the Bible also says God is our strength, a tested help in times of trouble, and I have found this to be abundantly true.

This all sounds rather self-righteous, as though I'd arrived. Far from it! As one writer put it, "Christians are not perfect—they're just forgiven."

What happened in that moment under the fir trees? I realized that when one ignores God's laws, the penalty is spiritual death, or eternal separation from God. But in recognizing my transgressions, asking divine help and changing my ways, I was assured of God's forgiveness. What a wonderful chance to make amends is available to all of us.

God is sovereign and I don't understand why He planned the world as He did, but I don't have to understand. Gradually I came to realize that God loved me (and every other person on earth) so much that He sent His son, Jesus, to earth so that at the proper time in history He might die on a cross. His death paid the penalty for my transgressions so I can spend eternity in heaven with God. My sins were thereby pardoned. But for the pardon to be effective I had to take the positive step of accepting God's love.

Earlier in my life, as a churchgoer I thought I *had* accepted God's forgiveness, and wondered why I had no real peace. But on that weekend at the Firs I realized what acceptance really meant.

When I was baptized at the age of ten, the minister asked me, "Do you accept God's pardon and take Jesus as your personal savior?"

Without fully comprehending, I replied, "Yes, I do." That was an important step. But for many years I had only an intellectual belief. My regular church attendance was just religious activity. I was still living for self, each decision based on what *I* could get out of it.

Under the fir trees that morning I totally surrendered to God's rule in my life. I hadn't understood what it meant to put my full trust in God. This is illustrated by the parachute that saved my life. The Boeing training showed me how to use it and I had an intellectual belief in the chute's effectiveness. When the real test came, however, I had to take a bold step of faith and put my full trust in the chute.

For nearly 30 years I'd believed intellectually that Christ died for my sins, but I wasn't willing to trust Him to direct my steps day by day. I had to make a total commitment; it was all or nothing. Now that I understood how vital it was, I could take that step.

I know the Bible says "God so loved the world that He gave His only son that whoever believes on him might have eternal life."[2] Although "believe" is the best available English translation, the original Greek word also means "to rely on, put full trust in." For these many years I'd "believed," without putting my full trust in a loving Father who wants to direct my steps gently in the way I should go. I had stubbornly resisted anything that I thought kept me from doing what would benefit *me*.

Now I began to put into practice the admonition, "Seek first His kingdom and His righteousness, and all these things will be given to you as well,"[3] and found it was true. I still don't have my own airplane, but the Lord has provided opportunities for me to fly many varieties of aircraft.

"The good man does not escape all troubles—he has them, too. But the Lord helps him in each and every one."[4] I don't pray to avoid trouble. I've had my share and then some. When I found myself in a stalling, diving Flying Fortress with some missing tail parts and no way to land the plane safely, I prayed for the Lord's help and He enabled me to parachute to safety.

When the going gets tough I take a deep breath, close my eyes and repeat my favorite Bible verse, "...they that wait on the Lord shall renew their strength; they shall mount up with wings as eagles; they shall run, and not be weary; and they shall walk and not faint."[5] I love this verse. It describes a very graceful flier, the eagle, and it reminds me of the ecstatic joys of flying. Most of all I like it because it is a promise from a loving and caring Father in heaven, and I know I can count on His promise. I've never failed to experience renewed strength upon repeating this verse and praying, "Father, make it come true in my life right now."

I am supremely thankful for the day I got on a new flight plan and soared above the turmoil of life into a commitment to Christ. God's strength enables me to survive the daily struggle.

In the following weeks I noticed a tremendous difference in myself, and I feel the change was obvious to others as well. It was not long after that when Ted Ayre, a Boeing engineer, told me some exciting news. As fellow members of a flying club Ted and I shared a fast 125 hp two-place Globe Swift with other participants.

"Marv, have you heard about Mission Aviation Fellowship?" Ted asked.

"No, what is it?"

"It's an organization in California. They have about a half dozen airplanes, mostly four-place Pipers. They furnish air transportation for missionaries in Mexico, Ecuador, and other third world countries. They say five minutes in one of their planes will take you as far as you can walk along a jungle trail in twenty-four hours, so it saves the missionaries a lot of time."

"Wow!" I said, "That's fantastic! How do I find out more about them?"

"They have a monthly newsletter. I'll have them put your name on the mailing list." Thus began my 36-year association with Mission Aviation Fellowship.

---

[1] Philippians 4:19 KJV

[2] John 3:16 RSV

[3] Matthew 6:33 NIV

[4] Psalms 34:19 TLB

[5] Isaiah 40:31 KJV

Chapter Fifteen

LAUNCHED INTO THE JET AGE

I'll never forget my first flight in the B-47 Stratojet bomber. We took off from Boeing Field heading south. A minute or so after takeoff, I looked back toward the airport. There wasn't a very good view because in that short time we had climbed to 3,000 feet and were miles from the field. The performance, compared to that of reciprocating engine planes, was incredible!

I was anxious to learn the technology which would qualify me to fly this wonderful new airplane. The B-47's were in production in Wichita, so Boeing sent me there to get checked out as a copilot. Before I made my first flight as a copilot I went to ground school to learn the various systems of the B-47—the hydraulic system, the electrical system, etc. They didn't have flight simulators for the B-47. The 707 was the first Boeing plane for which we had a simulator.

The B-47 jet made its first flight in 1947, ushering in a new era of transportation. Far more sophisticated and beautiful than anything Boeing had ever built, the design of the B-47 was triggered by General Electric's development of its first jet engine. I gasped in amazement when I first saw its sleek lines. The thin, 116-foot long wing was extraordinarily flexible and swept back at a rakish 35-degree angle. Hanging beneath the wing were pods containing six GE J-35 jet engines. The Stratojet could fly faster and higher than nearly every other airplane in existence. It could reach a maximum speed of 606 mph, while current non-jet airline planes were cruising at 300 mph.

Flying the Stratojet required faster reflexes and greater piloting skills than for reciprocating engine planes. On landing approach, the decision to make an emergency go-around had to be made earlier because the jet engines turned at 10,000 rpm, and took much longer to speed up to full power when throttles were opened. Even with a 10,000 foot runway, the pilot had to make a significantly more precise landing. If the approach speed was even five knots too fast, the pilot risked running off the far end of the runway. If the speed was five knots too slow, the pilot risked stalling if the air was turbulent.

In aerodynamic terms the plane was very "clean." It was like a sports car compared to a truck. It had so little drag that it was more difficult to decelerate on landing. To slow down more quickly, the pilot deployed a huge parachute attached to the tail. However, he had to wait to pop the chute until the speed had decreased to 125 knots (144 mph); otherwise the chute would tear loose from the plane.

On the ground, conventional planes can be steered by using the left wheel brake or the right wheel brake independently. The B-47 had a bicycle-type landing gear. Outrigger struts and wheels near the wingtip kept the plane from tipping and dragging a wingtip. The outrigger wheels had no brakes, so the main wheel brakes could only slow down or stop the plane, without steering it left or right.

The jet era brought new horizons to be conquered by pilots. In 1949 two Air Force officers flew their Boeing Stratojet cross country at an average speed of 607.8 miles per hour, breaking all existing coast-to-coast records. In 1951 Boeing tooled up for mass production of jet bombers—the most complex task the aviation industry yet had faced.

In June 1952 I was copilot on a B-47 flight at 26,000 feet when the No. 6 engine near the right hand wingtip exhibited excessive "choo choo" and flamed out. "Choo choo," like the sound of a train engine, describes the condition when some of the blades of the turbine engine stall and become ineffective. Fire broke out, with flames shooting out for 20 feet behind the engine. Pilot Rod Randall shouted over the intercom: "Fire on No. 6! I'm discharging the fire extinguisher!" The flames continued unabated.

"The fire extinguisher didn't work!" Rod's voice was tense. My stomach knotted and fear gripped me. If the fire weakened the wing structure enough to bend upward or break off the wing, we'd be unable to eject.

"I'm going to dive, and if that doesn't blow it out we'll eject," Rod announced to the crew. "Start through your ejection checklist, but don't eject 'til I give the word!" Immediately crew members started to go through the list: The B-47 had ejection seats, so first we would have to arm the cartridge that would expel us, then jettison the canopy, then pull the release lever that would eject us from the plane. Ejection seats were new with the jets.

We dived for an interminable time, although actually only a matter of seconds. I wondered whether the plane would hold together; if it failed structurally, we would not be able to eject.

"Thank God, it's out!" said Rod, as he gently pulled out of the dive.

Greatly relieved but still shaking, we radioed Boeing ground station and headed for home. Upon landing we found a hole one foot in diameter burned through the metal wing skin.

"Another minute or two of burning and we'd have lost the airplane," said John Turner, head of the structures department. "Your guardian angel was on duty!"

This proved to be the last really frightening incident in my Boeing career. By 1953, flight research began to slow down, and five test pilots were transferred to other Boeing jobs within a six month period. I became a technical writer and editor of pilots' manuals. Pilots filled these jobs because their flying experience enabled them to write instructions that were clearly understood by other pilots. During this phase of my career I edited flight manuals for the KC-97 and KC-135 tankers, C-135 military jet transport, B-52 bomber, 737 and 747 jet transports.

I'm sure all of the former test pilots at times missed the excitement of our earlier assignment, but there were advantages in a less stressful way of life. It was important to me to maintain my flying skills, however, and I continued my activities with the Boeing Employees Soaring Club. I enjoyed flying the club's Super Cub towplane and taking family and friends up in the sailplanes. One outcome of these flights is that my grandson, Jim Dillon, became a pilot for United Express and granddaughter, Carolyn Dillon, became a pilot for Alaska Airlines. I must confess that at times I yearned once again to climb into the cockpit of one of Boeing's bigger birds. I was therefore thrilled to receive a special assignment in 1970 which enabled me to do that very thing.

The Air Force cut orders by which I was to fly 20,000 miles around the Pacific in nine days, riding in the cockpit as an additional crew member of a C-135 jet transport. I listened to the intercom and radio while observing crews' use of the flight manual, checklists and performance charts. I answered their questions regarding any uncertainties they had about the instructions in these publications, and recorded any difficulties they had so that we could make needed improvements.

I went first to Travis Air Force Base near Sacramento, via commercial airline. My initial C-135 flight took me to Hickam Air Force Base in Honolulu. For one day I talked with flight and maintenance crews, gathering their squawks. I repeated this assignment in Tokyo and Manila.

There was no C-135 flight scheduled from Tokyo to Manila for a full week, so I reluctantly took a flight on a Douglas C-125, a plane which had acquired the unfortunate but accurate nickname of "old shakey." The airplane really did shake badly, and the four reciprocating engines and propellers were extremely noisy. I took advantage of the long, tedious flight to type a detailed draft of my trip report.

155

A free weekend in Manila gave me a welcome opportunity to spend some time with Mission Aviation Fellowship pilot Don Berry and his wife, Phyllis, who showed me much of the city. I was especially interested in Faith Academy, where missionaries' children from all over southeast Asia attend grade and high school.

My interest in Christian aid organizations had continued to grow since I first became associated with Mission Aviation Fellowship in 1952. Over the years Boeing was generous in allowing me time off occasionally to take part in special missions. After I became an editor, the excitement and spiritual rewards of those occasional ventures helped to take the place in my life of the challenging activities which my former work as a test pilot had provided. My association with these Christian organizations played an important role in helping me adjust to my departure from Boeing.

In 1970, the economic downturn made it necessary for Boeing to make a significant reduction in facilities and manpower. The loss of thousands of jobs had a drastic effect upon the community, and it was then that someone put up a billboard saying, "Will the last person to leave Seattle please turn out the lights." My employment continued for another two years, but the handwriting on the wall grew clearer, and in 1972, along with many other long-time employees, I was asked to take early retirement.

It wasn't easy to face the reduction in income, but an even greater consideration was the question of how I would now spend my time, at age 59, after a demanding and fulfilling working career. Looking back now, I see how fortunate I was that God had so arranged my earlier years that a transition into work with Christian organizations became the new and absorbing interest in my life. In providing the background for this transition, I should go back to my meeting with Nate Saint in 1952.

Chapter Sixteen

"CONQUERING JUNGLE BARRIERS"

That stormy November in 1952 brought more than the usual rain to our house in Seattle. Our modest home with four small bedrooms was to do double duty when the Nate Saint family of three joined our clan of five. Nate was the pioneer Mission Aviation Fellowship pilot among the human-head-hunting Jivaro Indians in the Ecuadorian jungle, and I couldn't wait to meet him. I paced in front of our living room window, stopped to look for their car, and wished they'd arrive. The mouth-watering aroma of frying chicken filled the house, as Laura prepared dinner for our company.

At last the doorbell rang and I hastened to greet our visitors. On the porch stood a slender man in a light shirt and tan slacks. I could see goose bumps on his bare arms from the nippy weather. His blue eyes sparkled and a wide grin displayed dazzling white teeth. I held out my hand. "You must be Nate."

His handshake was warm and firm. "You must be Marvin."

"Just call me Marv." I'd read a little bit about Nate, and I greatly admired his dedication in serving as a pilot for remote missionaries. Mission Aviation Fellowship furnished air transportation at that time for missionaries in six third world countries. (It currently serves 30 countries.)

Over his shoulder I could see a little girl watching us from the back seat of an old green Chevy panel truck with "Mission Aviation Fellowship" painted on the side. His wife looked our way from the front seat.

"Nate, let's get your family in here. You must be dead tired." He nodded and motioned to his wife. Marj was a strong, five foot two brunette, with large brown eyes, and a little upturned nose. She too had a wonderful smile.

Inside, with introductions concluded, I steered Nate into the living room until Laura could serve dinner. Their two-year-old Kathy and our three kids were getting acquainted in the family room while Laura and Marj chatted in the kitchen over last minute preparations.

"Dinner's almost ready," I said, "I'm so pleased that you're staying with us."

Nate didn't want to sit, but wandered about the room looking at our pictures. He stopped in front of a large colored photo of my old Flying Fortress. "Marv, I think you and I are going to hit it off!"

My thoughts exactly. Already I felt as though I'd known Nate a long time, and looked forward eagerly to helping him show his film to churches in my community. "Do you think tomorrow we could see your film?" I asked. "Conquering Jungle Barriers" was the story of Nate's work in Ecuador.

"Sure, Marv. We'll cut out, just the two of us. Then maybe we could take a look at churches and begin to set up our showings."

"No problem," I replied. "I've already worked out a schedule."

I was very interested in hearing about his work in Ecuador. "What kind of plane do you fly for the missionaries?"

"A four-passenger Piper Pacer. We installed oversize tires and brakes because the airstrips are so rough and short."

Just then Laura announced, "Dinner's ready." Our table conversation centered on Nate's experiences on this junket.

"How far did you drive today?" I asked.

"I figure about 430 miles. We got a late start—it's been a long day. It started raining as soon as we hit Washington."

By the time apple pie was served, little Kathy was beginning to nod off.

"We're all tired," Marj said. "We'd better turn in early."

Next morning after breakfast Nate set up his projector in the master bedroom because it was easily darkened. "Conquering Jungle Barriers" was a revelation to me. Nate's home-spun movie, spiced with humor, took me into the heart of the jungle. It opened my eyes to the loving, devoted missionaries Nate served and the primitive Quichua, Jivaro and Atshuara Indians for whom the missionaries ministered. The movie had many surprises.

In his film narration, Nate asked, "Do you know what jungle chewing gum is?" Then two grinning Atshuara Indians faced the camera, their bare chests daubed with red war paint. They each were enjoying a snack—a huge wriggling worm. "This is jungle chewing gum," said Nate, " the wriggley brand!"

The film showed that in the jungle, the most welcome sound was the approaching hum of Nate's engine. The missionary would be conducting his work for the afternoon—giving out some aspirin, treating a baby's fever, or planting a garden. Nate's plane was heard in the distance, and there would be a grand rush to check the airstrip. The missionary would hike over the strip for a final look at the surface, and when children and dogs were at a safe distance, the little yellow plane would approach and settle onto the turf. As the prop stopped turning the door would swing open and a sunburned, sandy-haired young man with an angular frame and flashing smile would hop out—Nate Saint, the man whose energy had revolutionized missionary life in the bush.

Nate would unload the cargo listed for that station, checking out loud the list which Marj had made out for him.

"Let's see: Meat, vegetables, ten gallons of kerosene, a broom, and the mail. Your prescription's in the mail sack. Guess that's it. How's it going, Jim?" Then he was off to the next mission station. As the movie ended I was suddenly whisked from the Ecuadorian jungle back to the U.S.

This was Nate's first visit to Seattle, so I navigated for him. In setting up his schedule for three and a half weeks, I had talked to most of the pastors of the various denominations. As we went from church to church, I introduced Nate to the pastors. The purpose of the film showings was to raise funds and solicit new pilots for Mission Aviation Fellowship. They were looking for full-time pilots, who needed to be dedicated to the Lord's work, as the small salary they made was never as much as could be made in commercial flying.

Each evening when we returned from a film showing, we'd have a piece of pie or cake and hot chocolate before going to bed. With a mischievous twinkle in his eye Nate asked, "Should we say grace for this? They tell me if it costs less than fifty cents, you don't have to!"

As their time in Seattle was drawing to a close, over another bedtime snack Nate surprised me by saying, "Marv, have you ever thought about joining Mission Aviation Fellowship?"

"I don't believe I qualify," I replied. "I am a Boeing test pilot, but I don't have an airplane mechanic's license." The latter was a necessary MAF requirement, considering the remote areas its pilots serviced.

"I wasn't thinking of your coming as a pilot, but as an administrator in our headquarters office."

"Hmm. I'll have to think about that."

"Can you take some vacation over the Christmas holidays and stay with us in L.A. to get better acquainted with MAF? Maybe you'd like to do a little volunteer work by way of getting to know some of the folks."

I was curious to know more about MAF and this sounded like a wonderful opportunity. The timing seemed perfect. Boeing always shuts down Christmas through New Year's Day. I also was able to use some of my 1952 and 1953 vacation time. Laura and I and the children drove to Los Angeles.

Marj Saint welcomed us warmly. "Nate and I are so glad to have an opportunity to return your hospitality." Their small house was sparsely furnished, but seemed very homey to us.

On his way to work in the hangar each morning, Nate dropped me off at Charlie Mellis's tiny south Los Angeles house which served as MAF headquarters. I helped with typing, filing and all kinds of menial tasks while getting to know the staff.

One day Nate said, "I've got a brainstorm that you can help me with. When missionaries are hacking their way through the underbrush they sometimes get sick or run out of food. If I could let out a bucket on a long cord and trail it behind the plane, I could fly circles around the people on the ground and by slowly decreasing altitude, maybe I could lower some medicine or food to the ground in the container. As far as I know, this hasn't ever been tried. Let's go see if we can make it work."

This sounded more exciting than working in the office. I was happy for the break. In a discount store Nate and I bought a small canvas bucket and 1500 feet of nylon cord. We wrapped the cord on a reel, tied the bucket (which we had filled with oranges) on the end of the cord, and installed it in a Piper Pacer. Nate said, "If this thing works, the container will settle down to the ground. I want you to be waiting on the airstrip to take out the oranges and give me a big hand wave so I'll know it's 'mission completed'."

He took off with his helper, Tom. As they were climbing to altitude, Tom reeled out the bucket and cord so it trailed behind the plane. Nate leveled out on reaching a thousand feet. Looking up, I kept turning as Nate expertly flew the yellow Pacer in a circling steep bank around me. Gradually he decreased altitude as the cord and the bucket described an inverted cone.

It came down lower and lower until I caught the bucket, removed the oranges and waved a thumbs up to Nate. Tom reeled in the line and Nate's bucket drop became a reality! The plan's success was exciting and I could hardly wait for him to land. When he climbed out of the plane I thumped him on the back and yelled, "You did it, Nate. You did it!" As we were discussing it with our wives that evening I said, "I'm thrilled to have helped make it work."

Nate was not only a highly skilled pilot; he was also a mechanic, carpenter, artist, published writer, speaker, photographer and inventive genius. That was not surprising, for his father, renowned for his design of stained glass windows, was the artist of the great north transept rose window in the National Cathedral in Washington, D.C.

Lives were saved as MAF pilots used Nate's famous bucket drop to lower medicine or food to people on the ground when there was no nearby airstrip. Nate installed a field telephone in the bucket and ran the wire up the cord to the plane so he could talk with people on the ground. The Air Force successfully used this system later.

On one occasion in Ecuador, missionary Frank Whiting, his wife and two children walked for three days from their mission station to the MAF base at the little town of Shell (where Nate and his family were based) to buy supplies and receive routine medical care. Their mission station had no airstrip.

As they were returning home, Nate made a point of flying over them on one of his cargo flights. As he rocked his wings in a friendly greeting, the missionary frantically waved a white towel and pointed repeatedly at his son, David, lying on the ground.

Nate lowered the telephone. With desperation in his voice, Whiting told Nate, "David was just bitten by a coral snake. Can you bring us some antivenin right away?"

"Will do! Sorry to hear it. I should be back in about 45 minutes."

There was not a minute to lose, as the coral snake's venom can prove fatal in a very short time. Nate headed for Shell, radioing Marj to have the antivenin ready. He landed, taxied up to the house without shutting down, and Marj handed him a package. Back in the air he found the Whitings and lowered the antivenin in the bucket.

Whiting retrieved the package and grabbed the phone.

"Thank you, thank you! Nate, we can't tell you what this means to us." When Nate learned later that David had survived, he said a prayer of thanksgiving.

Although Nate was deeply religious, he was not fanatic. Just being around him I sensed that God was a vital part of his life. In a most natural way, he would question, "I wonder how the Lord would have me do this." That kind of thinking was foreign to me, and I realized that something important was lacking in my life. My mind began to question how the Lord would have *me* handle problems that arose. Nate made a tremendous impact on my life and I spent a lot of time reflecting on his firm but gentle ways.

Nate told me that when he began planning his film he asked Charlie Mellis, MAF treasurer, for financial assistance. Charlie wrote back, "Sorry Nate, slides tell the story adequately and movies are much too expensive." Nate and Marj disagreed, and saved enough out of their small living allowance to buy a used movie camera. After seeing "Conquering Jungle Barriers," Charlie agreed it was indeed superior to slides. Although Nate knew he'd have to shoot at 24 frames per second to add an optical sound track, he chose to shoot at silent speed, 16 frames per second, because it gave him 50 percent more coverage for the same money. This required that someone narrate the film in person when it was shown.

Nate traveled from city to city showing his film. Sometimes he arrived barely in time for an evening showing after a tiring, long day's drive. He became frustrated because his fatigue caused him to miss several of the important punch lines as he narrated the story.

His solution was to tape record the narration and synchronize the film with it. One small problem: The film either got ahead of or fell behind the story line. With typical Saint ingenuity, he installed a resistor in the projector motor circuit which slowed the speed from 16 to 15 frames per second. By switching back and forth, he kept the film and tape synchronized.

As our four week visit with MAF drew to a close, I was asked for my answer: Would I leave Boeing to join MAF? I was strongly tempted. Sensing an abiding peace and joy in the lives of Nate and Marj, I felt that perhaps working with MAF would make me a better Christian.

Laura was not enthusiastic about my joining MAF. My test pilot job paid a good salary, and as was the case with many other Christian organizations, MAF salaries were quite small. We realized we couldn't afford private schooling, music lessons and other things for our children on an MAF salary. And from a very personal standpoint, I knew if I were to go to MAF at that time I'd never be able to own my own airplane. I wasn't prepared to close the door on my lifelong dream. With considerable reluctance, I decided that God was not calling me to leave Boeing for administrative work at MAF just then.

Back in Seattle, the phone rang. Grady Parrott, MAF president, was on the line.

"We're getting calls from people up there asking if they can show 'Conquering Jungle Barriers' in their churches. We can't send them the film and tape because only someone who knows the script intimately is able to keep it synchronized. You're the only one in Seattle who can do this. Would you be willing to show it in response to these requests?"

"I suppose I could," I replied. Nate's filming genius and his abundant and easygoing humor made the movie very popular. The requests for showings snowballed, and soon I was showing it once, twice or occasionally three times a week. The film is indeed a classic, which is still being shown forty years later, with the ingenious later addition of an optical sound track.

In my youthful exuberance, I neglected my wife and family. MAF required that I arrive at least 45 minutes early to get set up. This allowed time to change a projector bulb or splice a film if necessary and still start the show on time. Many times I asked Laura to have dinner ready early, and after gulping my food I dashed off, leaving the dishes and care of the children for Laura. There was no time for fun with my family.

With a pained expression and tears, Laura said, "I think you're spending way too much time showing Nate's film. It seems like you're never home. You should cancel some of your showings." I sensed her smoldering anger.

"Laura, I'm the only one who can show it. We can't let these people down who are clamoring to see it!" Laura reminded me frequently of my responsibilities at home, and eventually I cut back my schedule. Much later, I deeply regretted having spent so much time on this activity at my family's expense.

After I had been showing the film for a few months, Grady Parrott wrote, "You've been doing the work of an area representative, so we've just made you an official representative. Congratulations!" This was the beginning of a 36-year alliance with Mission Aviation Fellowship, which has provided me with adventure, challenge, and great spiritual rewards.

Chapter Seventeen

MISSION TO ECUADOR

Nate Saint and four missionary companions and their wives prayed for years for an opportunity to share the gospel with the Auca Indians of Ecuador, but it was extremely difficult to establish rapport with them. The Aucas have been described as the world's most savage, bloodthirsty killers. Many years ago, white traders purchased rubber from them, paying with beads and trinkets. Later, the traders took rubber without paying for it. Thereafter, every white man who ventured into Auca territory was killed on sight. This did not deter Nate and his companions from their attempts to befriend this isolated tribe.

The day came when Nate and his missionary companions felt it was time to begin delivering a weekly gift to the Aucas. Pots, pans, knives, and other useful items were delivered, using Nate's famous bucket drop. After the first of these weekly gift drops, the Aucas began fastening one of their hand-made baskets, with their gifts, onto the rope. The Indians sent back such gifts as smoked monkey meat and a live parrot. Once the gift-giving relationship had been established, the Aucas waved friendly greetings to the plane circling overhead on each weekly visit.

In November 1955 I wrote Nate that our newest family member, Larry, had just been born. On December 8, Nate replied, "Congratulations on the arrival of another man to garrison the Michael fort. May God bless and use him in what surely looks like the gravest epoch man has faced since the flood. When I look at our Philip I think that these little ones are particularly blessed of God, for it may be their privilege to lay down their lives for Christ's sake. These are terrible, yet wonderful times in which to be a witness on the world scene, aren't they?" The deep significance of those words didn't hit me until several weeks later.

Just one week before Christmas, Nate sat down at his typewriter to tell the world why the five missionaries were going to meet the primitive Aucas, just in case the five didn't come back. He wrote, "As we have a high old time this Christmas, may we who know Christ hear the cry of the damned as they hurtle headlong into the Christless night without ever a chance...May we shed tears of repentance for those we have failed to bring out of darkness.

"Would that we could comprehend the lot of these stone-age people who live in mortal fear of ambush on the jungle trail...those to whom the bark of a gun means sudden, mysterious death...those who think all men in all the world are killers like themselves. If God would grant us the vision, the word sacrifice would disappear from our lips and thoughts; we would hate the things that seem now so dear to us; our lives would suddenly be too short—we would despise time-robbing distractions and charge the enemy with all our energies in the name of Christ."[1]

After thirteen weeks of weekly gift drops, the missionaries felt it was time to meet the Aucas face to face. The five men planned their strategy as carefully as any military campaign. With meticulous care, on a Tuesday morning Nate flew one team member and parts of a prefabricated tree house into Auca territory, landing on a stretch of beach on the Curaray River. He made six more flights that day with other team members and more tree house parts. The tree house was assembled high in a tree for safety, in case they had misjudged the Aucas. Three of the fellows slept in the tree house. Nate and another man flew back to their base each night so as not to leave the plane vulnerable to an attack on the beach.

Three Aucas—a young man, a younger girl, and an old woman— visited the missionaries on the fourth day. They nicknamed the young man "George." Nate took George up for a flight over his village. Using Nate's bull horn, George shouted and waved to the villagers, his own neighbors. Thinking back to my own first airplane flight at age fourteen, I knew the wonder and excitement the young Indian must have felt as he looked down at his jungle home.

From the very beginning, the five men and their wives realized this project was dangerous. They knew that if their plans became widely known, other missionaries in the area might want to join them or even oppose them. Government officials might try to stop their operation, so strict secrecy was maintained. Only the five couples knew of the top secret project.

The following Sunday morning Nate flew over the village and radioed Marj at the appointed time of 12:30 p.m. By prearrangement the message was coded to maintain secrecy, in case others might be listening. Nate radioed, "I've spotted a commission of ten on the way from Terminal City. Looks like they'll be here for the early afternoon service. Pray for us. This is the day! Will contact you next at 4:30."

At 4:30 p.m. Marj eagerly turned on the radio in Shell. This was the moment the wives had been waiting for. Had the Aucas invited the men to follow them to their houses? What further developments would Nate report? Nate never called.

Next morning, Johnny Keenan, the other MAF pilot, flew over the site and saw the totally vandalized airplane and four bodies. It was believed that one of the men might still be alive in the jungle.

The initial radio announcement from Quito, Ecuador said, "Four of the five young missionaries involved in a highly secret project deep in the heart of the Ecuadorian jungle were speared to death by a group of Auca Indians." The news quickly spread worldwide with big headlines. The whole world was shocked by the tragic event. I was horrified. I had a gut feeling Nate would be the one to survive, and yet I had a gnawing fear.

A few days later a fifth body was spotted. So Nate, too, was dead! He had been due to return to the States on furlough in a few months, and I was eagerly looking forward to seeing him again. I was devastated at his death. I felt cheated. Why would God allow five outstanding young men in their prime to be so brutally massacred? Gradually, however, I reached the understanding expressed by Marj Saint when she said, "They lost this battle, but they gained the victory."

After the fifth body was sighted from the air, a rescue crew went in and buried the five missionaries. The world said that the lonely common grave on the Curaray River, guarded by the stripped MAF plane, was a symbol of failure. The news media, including the Christian press, were very critical of the five men for risking their lives. But this was no tragedy. It was a glorious triumph in God's plan. Because of the example of five dedicated missionaries, willing to lay down their lives to take the gospel to savages, thousands of men and women committed their lives to full-time Christian service.

Not all continued in full-time Christian work. But if only a fraction persisted in their service to God, that is many more than if the five Ecuador martyrs had not laid down their lives. During the intervening years hundreds of young people have chosen to work for MAF and other Christian organizations as the result of reading books describing these events.

Marj Saint ended her book, *Jungle Pilot*, with a letter to her children:

"The story of your father's life has now been written. A few years ago there would have been no need to write these things, but there came a day when I had to tell you our Daddy wasn't coming back to live with us— he had gone with four of his friends to live with Jesus in heaven...Your daddy wrote to our friends the Michaels only a month before he was killed, saying 'When I look at our children, I think that these little ones are particularly blessed of God, for it may be their privilege to lay down their lives for Christ's sake.' You see, what Daddy thought might be God's plan for you, became God's plan for him...Love, Mother."

Nate Saint, missionary pilot, innovator and martyr, touched many lives, not only because of his missionary work, but through the warmth and guidance he gave to all his fellow workers and friends. Throughout my 36-year association with Mission Aviation Fellowship his example always stood before me as a goal and an inspiration.

[1]Russell T. Hitt, *Jungle Pilot*, Zondervan Publishing House, 1959, p. 249.
[2]Ibid., p. 263.

Chapter Eighteen

SPECIAL DELIVERY TO SOUTH AMERICA

"We're ferrying three Helio Courier planes down south—delivering them to the Peruvian government in Lima," said Larry Montgomery. "Better come along and help us fly them." Larry was head of JAARS (Jungle Aviation and Radio Service) for Wycliffe Bible Translators. He was on a stopover in Seattle, and we had joined him for dinner at the home of a friend.

"Yeah, that would be nice," I replied, halfheartedly. Sure would be nice if he really meant it, I thought to myself, and if Boeing would let me have enough time off, and if...No use getting my hopes up. After dinner Larry showed us slides of the important work which JAARS accomplished.

JAARS pilots provide air transportation for Wycliffe Translators in many primitive countries. Wycliffe is a group of several hundred missionaries who convert native languages to writing and translate the Bible into those languages.

Later that night, as Laura and I were saying goodby to Larry he reminded me, "Better get your bags packed real soon."

Laura chimed in, "Well, you know, Marvin can't go unless I go too!"

"I think that could be arranged," he replied.

Next morning Larry phoned. "Because you're an experienced pilot and active with MAF you can be a real help to us in ferrying the planes down there." Now I realized he really meant it.

Quickly our plans evolved. Laura was indeed invited to go along, and Boeing was receptive to my request for time off. We spent several hurried days renewing passports, making airline reservations to Kansas, getting visas, and packing. Within the week we were at the Helio factory in Pittsburg, Kansas. Short, stocky Merrill Piper, a sharp pilot, would be the flight leader. Slender, quiet Ralph Borthwick would fly the second plane, and I would fly the third.

Helio officials briefed us thoroughly on this unusual airplane. Our wives listened in, and Laura said later, "They emphasized the safety features so strongly that I didn't feel my usual anxiety about flying in small planes."

This unusual four-seater plane has wing slots and flaps which help it make steep takeoffs and landings. It can fly as slow as 30 mph. The slow speed enables it to get into and out of small fields, particularly where the fields are surrounded by trees or other obstacles. Cruising speed is 140 mph.

After dinner on the second and final day of pilot checkouts, Merrill laid out the flight plan for the next day. This was to be the pattern for the entire trip: Because of frequent afternoon tropical storms, we would take off at daybreak and settle in for the day by mid-afternoon.

Merrill's fluent Spanish greatly speeded our passage through Customs and Immigration. For the most part, that is.

In Nicaragua we ran into a storm and had to back-track and land at an airstrip off the beaten track. As we taxied up and parked our planes we saw scores of soldiers sitting on benches around the outside of the un-imposing headquarters building. They held rifles, butts resting on the ground. We were apprehensive, wondering if we had been caught in a revolution. We had visions of spending the night in a dirty, uncomfortable jail. Merrill told us to stay by the planes, make no sudden movements, and he would check the weather reports and get our clearance to proceed.

He returned shortly. "We're going to be detained," he said. "Follow me into the building." On the way in he continued, "Don't talk very much among yourselves, and especially, don't say anything derogatory about the officials or the government. Many officials pretend not to understand English so they can listen for any negative comments." We promised.

We were released a couple of hours later. That evening Merrill explained, "I think they detained us hoping we'd offer them some money to get on our way. This happens quite often. Apparently they finally realized that we just weren't going to bribe them. We were lucky."

When we arrived in the city of San Salvador the hotel clerk asked $12 for a very modest room. In Mexico

City we had paid $2.40 for a lovely room with two large beds and private bath in a new, modern hotel. After some bargaining he lowered the price and escorted us across the street to the annex. One look at the crumbling frame building and we concluded he was shuffling us off to the Old World part of the hotel.

We learned sadly that what we'd heard about inexpensive vacations down South was true only in Mexico. From there on down, the prices were as high or higher than in the States.

In a little grocery store in San Salvador we found a package labeled "Mission Macaroni, Seattle, Washington."

At last we arrived at our destination. In Lima, Merrill took three top government officials for a demonstration flight. He climbed almost straight up, turned on a dime, and landed on a postage stamp. Deeply impressed, the Minister of War shook my hand and said, "Dat ees a truly remarkable earaplane!" Delivery of the planes to the government ended our eight-day, 41-hour flight from the Helio factory in Kansas.

Next day our party of eight departed from Lima, flying over the Andes mountains in a good old Douglas DC-3 on Fawcett Airlines. As we flew between 13,000 and 18,000 feet altitude, we sucked oxygen from a pipe stem connected to a rubber tube. We landed on a dirt strip at Pucallpa, in the heart of the Peruvian jungle. Wycliffe's plane, a Catalina, was waiting for us.

Several years earlier the president of Mexico was so impressed with the work Wycliffe was doing that he gave Wycliffe a war surplus amphibious Catalina. It was a large twin-engined flying boat with retractible wheels, which had been used by the U.S. Navy in World War II for long range anti-submarine patrol. Wycliffe's founder and president, Cameron Townsend, earlier had asked Mission Aviation Fellowship to fly and maintain the Catalina for Wycliffe. MAF's officers felt they should not be involved in operating such a large plane, whereupon Townsend organized JAARS to operate it.

After a five-minute flight we settled smoothly on the lake at Yarina Cocha, the Wycliffe jungle base. We toured the base with Townsend, who was affectionately known as "Uncle Cam." We saw part of the JAARS fleet of 17 planes, including the old amphibious Grumman Duck biplane which had been flown several years earlier by a Seattleite, Betty Greene, when she was hailed as the first woman pilot to fly over the Andes mountains. Betty was one of the founders of Mission Aviation Fellowship, and was its first pilot.

"Payload is very important in these jungle mission planes," Townsend explained. "That's why we like lightweight pilots. You can put in your application any time, Mr. Michael." I was tempted, but resisted. I still felt a strong loyalty to MAF.

We returned to Quito, Ecuador by commercial airline, and then traveled by bus to Ambato, along with numerous Ecuadorians, their pigs and chickens. MAF pilot Hobey Lowrance flew us in a small Piper airplane from Ambato to Shell, where the foot of the Andes mountains meets the Ecuadorian jungle. Hobey, in his forties, was thin, energetic and very much the professional pilot.

A former American Airlines captain, Hobey went to Ecuador to take Nate Saint's place after Nate and his four missionary colleagues were slain by the Auca Indians eighteen months earlier. As we approached Shell, I recalled with a pang of sadness that five years earlier Nate had invited Laura and me to visit him in Ecuador some time.

Because Shell receives 240 inches of rain annually, the humidity is unusually high. When we climbed into bed that evening and slipped between the sticky damp sheets it took us quite some time to drop off to sleep.

Next morning Hobey said, "I'm making one of MAF's regular three week gift flights to the Aucas today, and you can come along and see part of it."

"How are chances of flying over the beach on the Curaray River where Nate and the other four missionaries are buried?" I asked.

"I'm sorry," said Hobey, "because I know how much that would mean to you, but we don't like to fly low over Auca territory for any purpose except to drop gifts. We've worked hard for more than a year to build up our friendly relationship with them, and other flights might frighten or confuse them and destroy our good relationship. Besides, there's a real element of risk. We maintain our planes very carefully, but there's still a possibility of a forced landing in Auca territory. We really don't know what their reaction would be—it could result in another slaughter of white people." We willingly conceded!

A 20-minute flight with Hobey in the Piper Cruiser took us to Arajuno, the mission station nearest the Aucas. The little airstrip was carved out of solid jungle and surrounded by 100-foot towering trees. It would have taken at least four days to hike there through the jungle.

As we set foot on the airstrip, we were filled with awe. This was the spot from which the five men had taken off for the Curaray River to carry the story of God's grace to the Aucas.

Gifts were being flown to the Aucas every three weeks, with the hope that some of the natives might be encouraged to come out to the mission station for friendly contacts with the missionaries.

We helped Hobey take off the door of the little yellow plane and rig up the reel with 1200 feet of heavy nylon cord, preparatory to using the now-famous bucket drop invented by Nate Saint. Hobey and Dr. Wilfred Tidmarsh, the resident missionary at Arajuno, fastened a basket with a live rooster on the end of the cord. Hobey briefed me for my part. If the Aucas gave a gift in return, I was to run out on the airstrip when he returned, cut the cord while he circled overhead, and recover the gift.

We watched Hobey and Dr. Tidmarsh take off for the Aucas, then walked up to the house to visit Mrs. Tidmarsh. "How far away are the Aucas?" I asked. Pointing to the hill across the river a couple of hundred yards away, she said, "They live a few miles from here, but we've seen Aucas on that hill spying on us. My husband built an electric fence around our yard to give us some protection."

Before long a faint hum told us Hobey and Dr. Tidmarsh were returning. I raced out to the airstrip and squinted skyward. There was the cord trailing behind the plane, and yes, something was dangling on the end! Hobey slowed the plane, banked steeply into a circling turn, and gradually reduced altitude. The objects on the end of the cord neatly settled down to the ground.

Wild with excitement I grabbed the cord, cut it, and there in my hand was a dead squirrel tied neck and neck with a dead parrot. Incredible! This gift had been picked up from the Aucas only ten minutes flying time from where I stood.

When Hobey landed I asked, "Do you think there's any particular significance to the Aucas' choice of a parrot and squirrel as a gift?"

"I can't think of any reason for their choice," Hobey replied. "One of their recent gifts was a smoked monkey leg. They consider this a real delicacy, so we were delighted to think they would want to give us such a special gift."

"Did you eat it?"

"Oh no! But we felt it was a good indication of our growing friendly relations."

My assisting role at the completion of Hobey's gift flight brought back poignant memories of the day five years earlier when I had helped Nate Saint with the initial trials of his bucket-drop idea.

Laura and I had lunch at Arajuno while Hobey flew the Tidmarsh family to another station. Gazing at the hill across the river, Laura asked me, "Do you suppose there are any Aucas over there watching us?" I shrugged. We had read in the *National Geographic* that the Aucas were the most savage, bloodthirsty killers in the world. Missionaries questioned the statement, but that didn't lessen our apprehension. Two hours later the hum of Hobey's engine was a most welcome sound.

Many miles and a few days later we stepped down the ramp from an airline DC-7 in Seattle. As we re-entered civilization, we marveled at the impact of the airplane upon the Stone Age jungle Indians of Ecuador,

Peru and other countries around the world. Truly, as Nate Saint so aptly said, "These are wonderful times in which to be a witness on the world scene."

Douglas DC-3 flown in famine relief in Ethiopia, East Africa, 1975-1977, by Marvin Michael and crew.

Chapter Nineteen

FEED MY FLOCK

It was quiet as I sat reading in my Bellevue home in April of 1975. The telephone startled me. Dr. Mervin Russell, president of Mercy Airlift in southern California, was on the line. He headed a Christian organization chartered to fly food to starving people in third world countries.

"The famine in Ethiopia is critical and we'd like you down here in two weeks, ready to fly to Ethiopia and assume field director and pilot duties." This came as quite a surprise, as I had submitted an application merely to fill in for pilots who were on vacation. Laura and I discussed this new development and agreed we should accept the challenge. I hurriedly packed, leaving Laura to join me later.

On arrival in Ontario, California, I met Dr. Russell.

"I'd like you to help Doug, our mechanic, finish installing the auxiliary fuel tanks in the cabin of our DC-3 before we begin our ferry flight to Ethiopia," he said. "The jets fly polar routes directly from the U.S. to Europe, but we have to take the longer route over the north Atlantic."

A few days later we were on the longest leg of our trip, ferrying our 36-year old "Gooney Bird" from Sondrestrom, Greenland, to Reykjavik, Iceland. The weather in May was frigid and blustery, and headwinds were so strong that we continuously calculated our fuel supply, hoping we would not run out. At the same time we worried about the starving Ethiopians whose food had already run out. To make it worse, we expended additional precious fuel climbing to 13,500 feet to top the clouds.

The radio navigational aids in this forlorn section of the world were minimal. As a Boeing test pilot I had been accustomed to using the latest electronics, but our radio equipment for the most part was WW II surplus. If either of our two tired engines coughed and quit, our best hope was to ditch our heavily loaded plane between icebergs in the freezing North Atlantic. The odds for surviving such a ditching were near zero. Worried, we prayed it would never happen, while accepting it as a calculated risk.

We were dressed warmly and the cockpit temperature was tolerable, but the passenger cabin heater wasn't working. I wasn't piloting on this leg, so back in the cabin I crawled into my sleeping bag to stop shivering. As the hours dragged on and the engines droned, I was too cold and miserable to sleep and too drowsy to read. Through occasional holes in the clouds we saw nothing but snow and ice below.

After hours of discomfort, I went forward to the cramped cockpit to thaw out. At last we sighted Iceland on the horizon and our copilot let out an excited

"There it is!" The crew of four was jubilant, knowing now that we would make it. Tired and stiff after sitting nine hours, we were extra cautious in going through our landing checklist. The touchdown at Reykjavik jarred our bones, but as pilots say, any landing you can walk away from is a good one. We rushed back to the door, threw it open, ran down the steps and kissed the ground!

The next day on our flight to London I was intrigued by the odd-shaped green fields bordered by a row of trees or rocks. This was an unusual sight for a farm boy from Kansas, where fields are rectangular. We woke up next morning and took a Sunday sightseeing bus tour of London. At dinner in the hotel that evening Dr. Russell gave us some background on how Mercy Airlift had become involved with Ethiopia.

"Ato Shimelis Adugna is the chief commissioner of the Ethiopian Relief and Rehabilitation Commission. Incidentally, 'Ato' means 'Mr.' and in addressing each other, Ethiopians use 'Ato' with only the first name. Ato Shimelis invited us to bring our plane and assist in famine relief. When the communists deposed Emperor Haile Selasse, Ato Shimelis was the only one of the top sixty government officials who was not executed.

"Why was he spared?" I asked.

"Because he was the only one capable of going to the industrialized countries and soliciting money and food. The communists knew they had to provide massive famine relief if they were to avoid an uncontrollable uprising of the starving people."

By the time we landed in Cairo we'd had our fill of traveling and were eager to arrive in Ethiopia. On our flight to Addis Ababa the long stretch of desert across

Egypt and Sudan was broken only by a narrow green belt bordering the Nile. The scenery was boring. A sandstorm sharply reduced visibility and made navigation difficult. If we flew through the thick of the sandstorm, the engines would ingest the sand and be ruined, so we climbed to 15,000 feet where we avoided most of the sand. As we were at the high altitude such a short time, we didn't bother with oxygen. Before long we were skimming a few hundred feet above native grass huts on the Ethiopian plateau.

We were excited and grateful when we landed at Addis Ababa and taxied to the terminal building. As we disembarked, a waiting news cameraman pointed his camera at us. It was a pleasant surprise that His Excellency Ato Shimelis Adugna personally welcomed us to his country with hearty handshakes. We were impressed that this high Ethiopian official, educated in Britain, would take the time to come to the airport and host us at lunch. He spoke in perfect English and we were instantly drawn to this short, stocky and unassuming man, well-dressed in a black business suit. Later we learned that he was a low-profile Christian. As a government official, being an openly active Christian in communist Ethiopia would have resulted in his execution. That evening in the hotel lobby we watched ourselves with interest on the black and white television set as our arrival was announced on the evening news.

The entire ferry flight was a fascinating study in extremes. In Sondrestrom, although this was 1975, we paid $104 for two tiny rooms with folding bunk beds and no bath. It was smaller than an economy class cruise ship stateroom. A few days later, the price of our $3 per person rooms in Cairo was in stark contrast to the $104!

190

The temperature had been 52 degrees below freezing over Greenland, but in Khartoum, Sudan, we tossed all night long in a sweltering 120 degrees.

And still ahead of us would be the most devastating extreme of all—the sad spectacle of human beings reduced to skin and bones and dying of malnutrition, when just an airplane flight away there were well-fed humans who took an abundance of food as a matter of course.

We settled in quickly in Addis and looked forward eagerly to flying in famine relief. Shortly after arriving in Ethiopia my copilot and I flew three 5500 pound loads of corn to a refugee camp near Imi, a small village 300 miles southeast of Addis. We took along a five-gallon can of automobile gasoline because we were told that the only car in Imi had no gas. It was a British-built Land Rover assigned to the priest of the Ethiopian Orthodox Church, who worked under the direction of the federal government.

Ato Tamru Feyissa, who accompanied us on the initial flights, was Ato Shimelis' assistant. Tamru, who had a thin mustache and wore a green tam, was a kind, helpful Ethiopian with a warm heart. He had a master's degree from the University of California at Los Angeles, and was the liaison between Shimelis and us.

"Climb in the car, fellas," said Tamru. "We're going to borrow it and go out to the refugee camp."

Several miles from Imi we climbed out of the Land Rover, and a few men and boys, all showing severe effects of prolonged malnutrition, approached us. The men wore filthy rags. The boys, up to about the age of ten, were naked. The heat was stifling and the stench was terrible. Flies were everywhere and crawled all over their faces until shooed away. They gathered around to see whether we had any food for them, smiling weakly when Tamru assured them we had indeed brought food. I felt so sorry for their pathetic circumstance that I almost cried.

The heat and smells made me woozy and the sights were shocking. Many lethargic men, women and children sat on the ground around their tiny shacks, which were about the size of an umbrella tent. Grass thatch or animal skins covered a hemispherical frame of tree limbs. Holes gaped in the roofs of the huts. There were no windows, and just an opening for a door. Six to eight people slept on the dirt floor. Most of them seemed in a daze, not caring whether they lived or died, perhaps even hoping they'd die before sundown.

The tribal chief, a wrinkled old man in rags who was about forty but looked sixty, spoke while Tamru interpreted in excellent English. "Two years ago there were 5,000 people in this tribe, but 3,800 have died of starvation and disease. Now there are 1,200.

"A widow with five children died this morning," said the chief. "One of the children was a baby, only a month old. Her husband died of starvation a long time ago." When we were shown her orphaned children we could see that one of them was already near death from starvation.

We looked inside a small hut where a woman in rags lay starving. "She's probably not over 40," said Tamru. "If she received food right now it's doubtful she'd live, because she looks like she's too weak to swallow. Intravenous feeding might save her, but there's no money for that." The woman looked 60 or 70. Her breasts were just shriveled skin. She didn't move, but blinked feebly as we came close and took pictures.

We took photographs because we knew the necessity for getting this story before our community at home, in an effort to obtain additional help for these unfortunate people. Our photographing brought mixed reactions, however. Some of the mothers seemed to sense that our purpose in taking pictures was eventually to help rather than just to satisfy morbid curiosity, so they held their children for us to take pictures. Some children stood silent while others cried and turned away from our cameras.

As we moved farther into the refugee camp we saw little girls, two or three years old, who were naked. As fast as they came into view, their mothers drew them into their huts, out of our sight. Older girls wore panties. A few had ragged dresses. The tummies of many bulged, indicating malnutrition, worms or both.

"Worms could be killed with medication, but there's no money for medicine," Tamru explained. "Even if it were available, it wouldn't be given because the children would soon be re-infected. Worms could be wiped out only by massive health and sanitation education, but there's no money for that."

As we unloaded sacks of corn, a few kernels spilled on the ground. One of the refugees gathered up the kernals with the dirt, and scooped them into the cloth that he had wrapped around himself. Later he would separate the grain from the dirt. I couldn't help thinking of the affluent community in which I lived. How happy these people would be with just the garbage we threw away. God, why have you given me so much wealth? Why am I not one of these starving men wearing rags?

* * * *

Laura arrived in Ethiopia a short time after I did. She wrote home to friends:

"I've been here a month and can almost say I feel at home in this strange, beautiful and exciting land. Addis Ababa (which means 'new flower') is a bizarre mixture of old and new. A place of tall, silvery blue eucalyptus trees that provide fuel for the city; boys selling baskets they carry on their heads; huts and thatched roof tukuls in the shadow of well-spaced modern banks and government buildings, hotels and offices; and flower-decked wide boulevards of a metropolis. On narrow back streets, donkeys and women carry hay and firewood, and herds of goats bring traffic to a halt. Although Addis is 8,000 feet above sea level and near the equator, the climate is temperate and pleasant."

As we became more and more at home in Ethiopia, our friendship with Tamru flourished. Several weeks after our arrival he invited us to his house for dinner. He and his wife were upper middle class Ethiopians. Their house was a typical American style house, maybe two bedrooms. They dressed in European style clothes.

When preparation of the meal was nearly completed, Tamru's lovely five year old daughter brought a pitcher of warm water. Going from one to another, she held a wash pan underneath and poured water over our hands as we washed them. His darling little three year old daughter came right behind with a towel to wipe our hands.

We then sat down to a typical Ethiopian dinner of wat and injera. Wat is a highly spiced stew which comes in many varieties. We served ourselves with goat wat, hardboiled egg wat and vegetable wat. Injera is a huge pancake, twenty inches in diameter, made with tef, an extremely nutritional grain native to Ethiopia. We watched our hosts to see how to eat this unusual food. I tore off a large piece of injera for one side of my plate and dipped some wat from the serving bowl to my plate. Then I picked up some wat with a small piece of injera and ate it with my fingers. The food was very spicy, but cottage cheese was served with it, which cut the effect of the hot spice. With the meal we drank hot tea. After dinner, our hosts repeated the hand washing ceremony. As we sat around after dinner, Tamru described his people and related an interesting legend.

"Ethiopians are not negroid; they are semitic. They don't have the wide nose and large lips of the negro. Ethiopian legend has it that after creating the world, God was lonesome and began to think about creating man. In order to make a man he fashioned a loaf in his own image, gave it two arms, two legs and a head. Then he put it in the oven to bake. When it came out it was quite white, not baked enough for God's taste. He threw it northward, and it became the white race."

With a big smile and a twinkle in his eye, Tamru continued: "On his second attempt, the baking time was too long and the bread came out burned. God threw it toward the south and the black race was born. Having learned from his two previous experiments, God then baked a loaf which turned out to be a beautiful brown. This was the Ethiopian, and God placed him on the top of the world close to his heart."

Later Laura again wrote home to our friends, but on a different note:

"Everywhere on the streets of the city are the street beggars, the blind, the crippled, the emaciated women with silent babies tied to their backs. The only English word that many Ethiopians know is 'hungry.' Gently but pleadingly they stretch out their hands chanting 'hungry, hun-

gry.' As the Ethiopian Herald put it, these are 'the wretched of the city.' Instinctively you shut your eyes, hoping things will be different when you open them, but they aren't. Hunger crowds upon you mercilessly. Their looks of entreaty will always be a part of us.

"At first we gave small change to the beggars. Their grapevine worked fast, for soon scores of beggars besieged us as we walked down the street or braked our car at a traffic light. We stopped handing out money, but our consciences bothered us. Then we learned of an expatriot mission which sold meal tickets for 25 cents U.S. through the churches. All but the professional beggars gladly accepted these tickets, which they exchanged for a meal at the mission soup kitchen."

Later we flew to the southern famine area, expecting to be away only one day. That afternoon we were surprised by a sudden record-breaking cloudburst along the Wabi Shebele River, where there had been almost no rain for four years. We were grounded for two days at Dr. Donald McClure's mission station in Gode until we could get through the mud to the airport. Dr. McClure had been working in Africa for 50 years. He'd helped me upon my arrival in Ethiopia and many times since. Often he'd said we were welcome to drop in for a meal or stay overnight any time. While waiting for the mud to dry, news came by short wave radio that floods had left many people hungry and homeless in Kelafo, a short distance to the southeast.

At the Gode airport, we stuffed the plane full of huge burlap sacks of bread and removed the rear entry door from the cabin. On reaching Kelafo we made a low pass over the center of town, the one spot for miles around that was not flooded. Since it was the only possible place to drop the bread, we circled the town, lining up for our first drop.

Approaching the area, we were stunned to see three men hurrying into the clear area, waving excitedly at us. If a sack of bread were to hit one of them it would kill him. In a split second we made the dreadful decision. It was a chance we had to take. Out went four sacks, all we could manage to shove out the narrow doorway during the short run. On our second run, the men were ripping open the sacks, utterly oblivious to the fact they were in the center of the target area. Now other people were arriving. Again, out went four sacks with a prayer that somehow they would miss those below. The last sack went out on the fifth run and we headed for home, wondering whether sacks had hit anyone on our final run. Later we heard that miraculously, not one person had been hit.

The airstrip at Kelafo was under three feet of water. In subsequent operations we brought in supplies to the old abandoned airstrip above the town. An Army helicopter shuttled them to the flooded areas.

The floodwaters rose in just twenty minutes, so swiftly that three Sudan Interior Mission (SIM) women barely escaped. They spent three harrowing days and nights perched on a large rock in the middle of the city, sweltering in the midday heat and shivering through the cold of night. On the third day a SIM man we had flown in from Gode rescued the women. He borrowed a rowboat and took them from the rock to the edge of town, where they walked up the rising terrain to the abandoned airstrip on which we had landed. They were greatly relieved and thankful when we flew them to Addis. Later we were shocked to learn they had been raped while stranded on the rock. The SIM director issued a sharply worded protest, but the perpetrators were never caught. What started as a one-day trip for us ended in eight days away from home. Thereafter, we carried toilet articles and a change of clothes on all flights!

Laura and I lived in a tiny government-owned apartment in Addis. Ethiopian meat and canned vegetables were tough and tasteless. Imported ham was $18 a pound. As volunteers we received just enough money to cover our living expenses. When I had to stay overnight in a downcountry seamy hotel, I took along a spray can of bug killer to rid the room of bedbugs and lice. We were continually frustrated by waiting hours to have our plane refueled and loaded with food. Time was meaningless to the Ethiopians. Despite the frustrations, seeing the smiling faces of the starving people as we brought food made it all worthwhile. Our reward was a joyful feeling of fulfillment, far beyond the satisfaction that my work as a Boeing test pilot had brought me.

Marvin Michael with His Excellency, Ato Shimelis
Adugna, Chief Commissioner of the Relief and Rehabilitation Commission of Ethiopia. Relief Commission logo
is painted on the DC-3 famine relief plane to preclude
hostile action by downcountry nationals. 1975

Chapter Twenty

TROUBLE IN GODE

On a Sunday morning in March 1977, a tap on my shoulder startled me as I sat in a Sunday School class in the International Church in Addis Ababa. Lindsay Nicholls urgently beckoned me to the back hall. He was the administrator for the Sudan Interior Mission.

"Trouble in Gode," he said. "Just got a radio message saying, 'send evacuation plane immediately.' No other details."

My heart pounded and my stomach churned as I imagined a guerrilla attack.

"Gode's an Ethiopian military base," I said. "I've flown relief supplies there. It takes 72 hours to get clearance from the defense department. We can't get a plane out there today."

"Gode is also a mission station with about thirty of our people," said Lindsay. "We've got to try today."

"It's Sunday," I reminded him. "All government offices are closed."

"Yes, but we've got to give it a try."

"You're right, we do."

My mind shifted to flight planning. Gode lay two and a half hours southeast of Addis, making round trip air time five hours if everything went perfectly. It might require half an hour ground time for the evacuation. Since the government prohibited night flying, we'd have to be back on the ground by sunset, which was always 6 p.m. here close to the equator. We needed to be airborne by 12:30 p.m.

I glanced at my watch. It was 10:30 a.m. No way could we be in the air in two hours! It took up to six hours to refuel the plane for a scheduled weekday flight. An unscheduled flight? On Sunday? Mission impossible!

Then I remembered that Dr. Donald McClure had started the mission at Gode. He'd helped me upon my arrival in Ethiopia and many times since. Dr. McClure had spent 50 years working in Africa. I admired this veteran missionary as much as any man I knew. Surely I could challenge the impossible for the sake of Dr. McClure's work! As the person in charge of the Mercy Airlift operation, only I could order the plane to go on this mission.

I sped to our Ghion Hotel apartment and started phoning, dispatching two mechanics to refuel the plane. Two weeks earlier I'd begun shutting down Mercy Airlift in Ethiopia because guerrilla warfare made flying too dangerous. My regular copilot had returned to the United States. Who would be my copilot? Suddenly I thought of Ron Smith, a veteran USAID pilot stationed in Addis Ababa. I had seen a guerrilla's bullet hole in his plane, so I felt his experience in dealing with this element would be helpful. I called Ron and told him I wanted him to go with me on an emergency mission.

"I was supposed to fly to London today," he said in his soft-spoken Texas drawl. I caught my breath. He continued, "But that flight was cancelled...I'll go. What time?"

"Meet me at the plane at 12."

I couldn't reach the Relief Commission chief or his assistant, so I called the U.S. Embassy to put in motion the process of getting our clearance. We'd be in deep trouble with the communist government if we took off without proper papers. The Embassy official was doubtful he could get through to the right people. "But we'll jump into action," he said. Fifteen phone calls and an hour and a half later we had our clearance to Gode! Time was growing very short.

I grabbed my flight bag and raced to the airport. Lindsay Nicholls met me there and said, "The plane is fueled and ready to go."

"I can't believe it!" I said. "They must have convinced the fuel man it's a serious emergency." The Ethiopians had such a different sense of time that I rarely succeeded in getting them to hurry. Lindsay and I ran together toward the plane.

"We notified the evacuees to be at the airport in Gode by 2:30," said Lindsay.

When we reached the plane Ron Smith was already there. "Smitty," I said, "You have a guerrilla bullet hole in your plane. What should we be prepared for if we run into an ambush?"

"Your guess is as good as mine," he replied. "I don't know where I picked up that bullet. Lucky it missed the gas tank or I wouldn't be here."

We climbed in, buckled into our seats and took off from Bole International Airport in Addis at 1:03 p.m.. With this delayed takeoff there was no way we would be able to return before sunset as required, but we took off immediately and made further plans in the air.

"Smitty, if I bring this plane down safely, you stay at the controls and keep the right-hand engine running so we can take off at the slightest sign of an ambush."

"Okay, Captain."

"I'll throw open the main entrance door and let the evacuees in. There are only four seats in the back. The rest will have to sit on the floor. I'll shut the door when I've counted 21 people."

Then I remembered that soldiers guarded the Gode tower, although military planes weren't regularly stationed there. Because our radio operated on a different frequency than theirs, we would have no means of contacting the tower on our arrival. "I hope the Ethiopian officials in Addis notified the soldiers that we're coming, so they won't try to shoot us down," I said.

"I don't know if that got done," Smitty responded.

Air turbulence cut off our conversation. Then I spotted the Wabi Shebele River and I knew we were nearing the airstrip.

"It's 3:30. We're an hour behind schedule. They probably gave up," I said.

"I don't see any activity down there," Smitty said.

"If the people are hiding 'til we land, we've got big trouble. I'll have to taxi off the runway to an apron to pick up passengers here. That means we can't position ourselves for quick takeoff." My stomach tightened. Suddenly I caught sight of people racing toward the airstrip. They had given up on us and started home. When they saw us coming in to land, however, they turned back to the field.

"Marv, we gotta get out of here as quick as we can." Smitty's voice trembled.

I couldn't respond—I had to pay attention to my landing. The tires hit the runway, I braked, turned around and taxied toward the crowd. Every second counted. Turning the controls over to Smitty, I unbuckled my seatbelt and stumbled toward the main entrance door as he brought the plane to a stop. I grasped the release latch and felt a blast of searing heat as the door burst open. The crowd surged toward the plane. We couldn't possibly take this many. Oh my God! What do I do now? Who was in charge here? Anybody? An Ethiopian man came up the steps first.

"One." I counted. "Is Dr. McClure here? Where's Dr. McClure? Two, three, four..."

"See Don Junior," the man shouted back. Evidently Dr. McClure's son was among the crowd.

"Fourteen." A woman hobbled up the steps with a large blood-soaked bandage on her leg. With dismay I recognized her as Pam Smith, wife of Graeme Smith, a World Vision agriculturist I had met in Gode. Her children clutched at her dress as her husband helped her up the steps. I anxiously watched for any sign of guerrillas.

"Seventeen. Where is Dr. McClure? Is Dr. McClure's son here?" No answer. "Twenty-one. No more. No more!" I pushed people back but four more squeezed through before I could get the door closed. About ten people still stood on the apron, strangely stoic, silent and passive. Their fear of another guerrilla attack showed in their faces. I felt painfully sorry for them, but couldn't help them. After latching the door I yelled. "Sit down. We're taking off right away!" and pushed my way to the cockpit.

"We're heavily loaded," I said to Smitty, as we buckled up.

"Nineteen minutes on the ground, sir."

"You all set for takeoff?" I asked.

"All set."

The plane lumbered down the runway. I watched the desert slowly slide past, wondering if the guerrillas would come running out. The extreme heat severely reduced engine power, and our heavy load further restricted airplane performance. The end of the runway seemed much too close. There were no runway markers to help me judge whether to abort the takeoff. It didn't seem an option anyway.

"God help us!" I gasped. I thought we were going to crash in the desert. The wheels reluctantly lifted off the hot tarmac just yards before the end of the runway. It took all of my concentration to coax the plane into the air.

"We made it!" said Smitty.

I wiped sweat from my brow. "We'll never get back to Addis tonight," I said, "We'll have to try to make Dire Dawa. It's forty minutes closer than Addis. I know the airport."

"Go for it," said Smitty.

"You fly," I said. "I've got to find out what happened to Dr. McClure. Don Junior was one of the last ones to board. He can tell me what happened last night."

"Yes sir," said Smitty, always the professional. But I saw the tears well in his eyes. I too feared the truth about what had happened at Gode. But I had to know.

I picked my way through the people sitting on the cargo floor. Men and women lined the sides of the cabin, leaning their backs against the wall. Children and some adults sat in the middle. They carried a few possessions tied in squares of cloth, and seemed frightened and subdued. When I reached the rear of the cabin I sat down on the floor by Don Junior, who, like his father, was an agricultural missionary. He taught the Surma tribesmen of southwest Ethiopia how to raise crops and care for a breed of cattle superior to their scrawny ones. On one of my flights to Gode I loaded up twenty head of cattle from Dr. McClure and flew them to Don Junior in Surma.

"What happened last night?" I asked.

Don's face looked strained. His voice choked when he tried to speak. He cleared his throat and began again. "About 1:30 this morning I heard a loud pounding on our bedroom window. A man yelled for Dad to come outside, so we got up and went out. About twenty Somalis were waving rifles and their ringleader yelled, 'McClure, give us $5,000.' Dad went into the bedroom, came out and handed the man about $150 and said, 'I don't have $5,000.'"

"How do you think the guy knew your dad's name?" I asked.

"I figure he must have been one of the men the Relief Commission hired to unload food stuff here on the compound. Somehow they knew there was $5,000 in the World Vision safe. About that time Graeme Smith heard the commotion and joined us." Don stopped for a moment and swallowed hard.

"Some of the bandits went to the other side of the house to get to the safe. Those who stayed with us argued among themselves." Don paused. "Suddenly the leader turned and fired several shots at the three of us, point blank. He couldn't have been more than ten feet away. We all fell to the ground, and they kept on arguing. When I realized I hadn't even been hit, I jumped up and ran for the bridge a half mile away."

"In the dark?" I asked.

"There was just enough moonlight for me to see. I knew soldiers guarded it day and night, and I figured they'd help us. But when they heard me, they started shooting, even though they couldn't see me. I dropped down and dug a foxhole as fast as I could, and waited. At daylight I made my way cautiously back to the compound, but the bandits were nowhere around. Graeme told me Dad had been the only one shot. He died instantly." Don's voice broke with a sob, and he dabbed at his eyes with a handkerchief. "We buried him right there on the compound."

I put my arm around Don Junior and let my tears join his.

I moved over to see if Graeme could talk. He too was suffering from shock and fatigue.

"Mike," he said, "when I heard those shots, point-blank, I thought we'd all die. But as I lay there listening to them argue, I was amazed they'd missed me completely. I figured if I lay real still they'd think I was dead and leave me alone." He stared straight ahead, in numb disbelief.

Then he went on, "After they left, I heard my kids crying and ran to see how they were doing. Pam told me the bandits routed her out of bed and asked her where the safe was. She said they tried to shoot the dial off, which was real scary, with bullets ricocheting all around. When that didn't work, they were boiling mad and got the kids out of bed and were getting ready to mow 'em all down."

"Oh no! That's horrible!"

He hesitated. His right hand clenched and unclenched. He continued. "When the bandits with Pam heard the shots being fired at us on the other side of the house, they must have thought they were being surprised by Ethiopian soldiers. They panicked and fired random shots as they took off. One of the bullets hit Pam in the leg. We've got to get her to the doctor as soon as possible. If the sound of gunfire hadn't frightened them off, they would have shot my whole family in cold blood." Graeme shuddered and shook his head.

The beloved Dr. McClure was laid to rest in a shady spot in the garden, in the country he called home, among the people he had loved and served so long. Half the population of Gode, sobbing and in tears, listened that morning as Don Junior explained simply but eloquently that his father's work on this earth was done and he was ready to go.

Tears filled my eyes as Graeme told the story. Dr. McClure's tragic death likely saved the lives of others who would have died if the bandits hadn't been frightened away. He would have been seventy-one in a few days, and had already packed to leave Africa for the last time. I remember him clearly as he was when I last saw him, laboring up the sloping cabin floor of our DC-3 as he carried 100 pound sacks of cement on his shoulder.

I headed back for the cockpit, but Don Junior stopped me. "Marv," he said, his voice trembling, "when we get to Dire Dawa I should call Addis and tell Mom the news, but I can't! I know I'll break down. Could you call Laura and have her go tell Mom, and stay overnight with her?"

"Of course. I'm sure Laura would be glad to do it," I replied. I checked my watch anxiously as we approached Dire Dawa and the 6 o'clock deadline.

We landed just three minutes before the airport closed at 6:00. It was an enormous relief. The Sudan Interior Mission housed some of our passengers and the rest stayed at a hotel. We flew in to Addis the next morning, where we were greeted by a joyful, noisy welcoming party of friends and relatives.

But for me, it was a very sobering experience. My friend Don, the ideal missionary—loving, generous, talented and always ready to help—was gone. I would miss him for a long, long time. I recalled that as we were scrambling to leave Addis on our rescue flight to Gode, I hadn't thought there was any possibility we could complete this mission. But we had flown into Gode against impossible odds and by the grace of God, we made it. In Africa I learned about adventure and heartbreak and challenge.

During the years that have passed since our sojourn in Africa, Laura and I have followed with intense interest the many changes that have taken place there. It has been heartbreaking to see that famines continue to take their toll both in Africa and in other parts of the world. We did have the satisfaction of knowing that our mission saved some lives at a time when our help was desperately needed, but unfortunately the need continues.

Although we are now in our eighties and no longer able to volunteer our services as active participants, we thank the Lord that He continues to inspire younger persons to spearhead relief projects. Our prayers are also with the missionaries whose efforts to better the lives of those in third world countries continue in the spirit of men like Doctor Donald McClure.

My earlier experiences as a pilot have brought some rewarding associations in my senior years. A few days after my 80th birthday I flew a Piper Super Cub as pilot-in-command. Thus I became a member of the UFO organization (United Flying Octogenarians). My brief ownership and assembly of a Waco airplane and assembly of an OX5 engine qualified me to become a member of the OX5 Aviation Pioneers, whose members must have owned and/or maintained and/or flown an OX5-powered airplane prior to 1940. More recently I was inducted into the OX5 Aviation Pioneers Hall of Fame in recognition of my contributions to aviation through my work at Boeing.

My faith and trust in Jesus Christ empowered me to achieve these accomplishments. They serve only to bring honor to Him.

Chapter Twenty-One

HEROES

Our lives are touched by others in a profound manner which it seems to me must be arranged by divine guidance. Looking back I can see that at crucial points along the way I encountered an outstanding person whose influence would deeply affect my life. I was able to benefit from the role models who were placed before me because I was open to their ideas and willing to change my own ways if necessary. The same situation exists in my relationship with God. I need continually to listen for that "still small voice."

I need to be willing and eager to ask His advice and help in all things, and I need to be ever watchful for the opportunities He gives me to offer others the help and encouragement they need.

Charles Lindbergh was my earliest hero. His daring deed captured my imagination, playing a major role in my choice of aviation as a career and lifelong interest. My admiration for him has not diminished over the years. I have visited the Smithsonian in Washington D.C.

on several occasions, where his Spirit of St. Louis is on display. On each visit I have marveled at the courage and pioneering spirit it must have taken for 24 year old Lindy to cross the Atlantic in that tiny plane, equipped with a single 225 horsepower engine. To put this in perspective, Boeing's 747 airliner with its four engines produces the equivalent of 250,000 HP.

As a young man when I was at the crossroads seeking the path which could lead me to my dreamed-of career in aviation, another hero arrived. Eddie Allen reached toward me with a helping hand which also was to alter the course of my life. My tremendous respect for him led me to strive to make my own contribution in aviation and as a human being. I have kept before me as a goal the words he wrote to me so long ago concerning "...the grand struggle against big odds toward an achievement."

When my spiritual growth became my guiding influence I was destined to meet someone who was indeed well-named—Nate Saint. It was obvious to me from the time we met that here was a man who walked a close walk with the Lord. During the few years I was privileged to be his friend I gained a great deal, not only in finding ways to use my flying skills for the glory of the Lord, but in learning to seek God's guidance continually in every aspect of my life. Nate and his fellow MAF pilots flew in and out of many short, rough jungle landing strips risking their lives to deliver medicine and supplies. In reality, every MAF pilot is a hero.

In Ethiopia I can still see seventy year-old Dr. Donald McClure carrying 100 pound sacks of cement up the sloping floor our DC-3. Gracious, loving, generous, hospitable Dr. McClure was a hero and a tremendous inspiration for me.

214

We never know what person is just around the corner who will play a leading role in our own development. And we never know whose life we ourselves may favorably affect, so that in some small way we too may become someone's hero.

One of my heroes is a young man I never met, but with whom I share a deep bond—our love of flying. Pilot Officer John G. Magee, Jr., who died in World War II, left a wonderful legacy. Aviators everywhere acknowledge that this young poet who died too soon captured the true essence of the miracle of flight in his classic poem:

HIGH FLIGHT
John Gillespie Magee, Jr.

Oh, I have slipped the surly bonds of earth,
And danced the skies on laughter-silvered wings;
Sunward I've climbed and joined the tumbling mirth
Of sun-split clouds—and done a hundred things
You have not dreamed of—wheeled and soared and swung
High in the sunlit silence. Hov'ring there
I've chased the shouting wind along and flung
My eager craft through footless halls of air.
   Up, up the long delirious burning blue
I've topped the wind-swept heights with easy grace,
   Where never lark, or even eagle, flew;
And, while with silent, lifting mind I've trod
The high untrespassed sanctity of space,
Put out my hand, and touched the face of God.

"High Flight" by John Gillespie Magee, Jr. New York Herald Tribune (February 8, '42)

GLOSSARY OF
AVIATION TERMS

Aeronca C-3: Two-seat "Bathtub Aeronca," wire-braced wingspan 36 ft, gross weight 875 lbs., cruising speed 65 mph, landing speed 35 mph, rate of climb 450 feet per minute, range 200 miles, Aeronca E-113 engine.

Aeronca E-113 engine: Two cylinders, 36 hp, single ignition. Later engines had two spark plugs per cylinder for greater reliability and lower fuel consumption.

Aeronca K: Two-seat strut-braced high wing monoplane, the successor to the Aeronca C-3. Early models had 36 hp engine; later models had 40 hp engine.

aerodynamics: The study of the motion of air and other gaseous fluids, and of the forces on solids in motion relative to such fluids.

ailerons: Control surfaces on the trailing edge of the wing, near the wingtip. They cause the plane to bank, i.e., rotate around the roll axis. They are controlled by turning the control wheel left or right, or moving the control stick left or right.

airspeed indicator: Indicates speed relative to the air.

altitude, high (This book):   Any altitude between 25,000 and 40,000 feet.

B-17G Flying Fortress: 4 Wright Cyclone 1200 hp engines; B is the Air Force designation for bomber. Wing span 103'-9", gross weight 48,726 lbs., top speed 302 mph, cruising speed 210 mph, range 3750 mi., bomb load 4,800 lbs.

B-29A Superfortress: 4 Wright Double Cyclone 2200 hp engines; wing span 141'3", gross weight 120,000 lbs., top speed 363 mph, cruising speed 220 mph, range 5830 miles, bomb load 20,000 lbs.

B-47 Stratojet: Six General Electric J-35 engined jet bomber. First flight was in 1947. Wing span 116 feet, wing sweepback 35 degrees. Bicycle landing gear with steerable front wheels. Outrigger struts and wheels near the wingtips keep the wings level. Maximum speed 608 mph. Crew: Pilot, copilot and bombardier.

B-50 Superfortress: A much improved B-29. 4 Pratt & Whitney Wasp Major 3500 hp engines; wing span 141'3", gross weight 164,500 lbs., top speed 400+mph, cruising speed 300 mph, range 4,000+ miles, bomb load 28,000 lbs.

Boeing 247D: Ten passenger twin-engined cantilever low wing monoplane. Retractible landing gear. Span 74'0". Cruise speed 189 mph. 550 hp Pratt & Whitney Wasp engines. First flight in 1933. Production limited to 75 because the Douglas DC-2 came out soon after, with superior performance.

Boeing 307B Stratoliner: Four 1,100 hp Wright Cyclone engined 33 passenger airliner. Cruise speed 220 mph. Outstanding feature was the first use of cabin pressurization for passenger comfort. The Stratoliner used the same wing, tail and powerplant as the B-17. First flight was in the late 1930s.

bank: To incline an airplane laterally. Right bank is to incline the airplane with the right wing down.

bombsight: An instrument which enables the bombardier to accurately drop the bombs on the target. The Norden bombsight was developed in the 1940s for use on the B-29 and other planes.

boundary layer control: Technique of channeling airflow around a wing to reduce stall speed and increase maximum speed. Early tests sucked turbulent air from the top surface of the wing into the interior of the wing.

C-97 Stratofreighter: The cargo version of the B-50. The double deck fuselage is substantially larger than the B-50 fuselage. The KC-97G tanker version with four 3500 hp Pratt & Whitney Wasp Major engines, cruised at 300 mph. The C-97 was redesigned to make the Stratocruiser passenger airplane.

cabin: The space in which the flight crews and passengers are housed. In contrast, an open cockpit houses pilot and passengers in an opening in the top of the fuselage.

cantilever wing: A wing having interior bracing with full-depth spars instead of external strut or wire bracing.

Caterpillar Club: Members are airmen who saved their lives by parachuting from a disabled aircraft. Paratroopers and sky divers are ineligible; they didn't have to bail out to save their lives. Caterpillars spun the silk from which the early parachutes were made, hence the name.

catwalk: On the B-17, a narrow bridge about ten inches wide which runs through the bomb bay in the center of the fuselage, connecting the rear compartment with the cockpit.

Civilian Pilot Training Program (CPTP): In the early 1940s the government paid civilian flying schools to train thousands of young people to fly as WWII loomed.

climb speed: The airspeed during the climb phase of flight. Generally it is considered to be the speed which results in the maximum rate of climb.

cockpit: The space which houses the flight crew, as distinguished from the cabin which houses the passengers and flight attendants. An "open cockpit" is an opening in the top of the fuselage, which houses a pilot or passenger. It usually has a windshield.

cold-soaked: The airplane has been exposed to extreme cold for a minimum of approximately four hours, usually at altitude.

compass, magnetic: Compass which relies on the earth's magnetic field to indicate direction. It is unreliable near the north and south poles. Because the floating compass is encased in liquid, the reading swings back and forth in rough air, making it difficult or impossible to read.

control stick: Performs the same function as a control wheel. One use of control stick is on the aerial refueling boom. Control wheel is now used on most airplanes.

control surface: A movable surface, e.g., aileron, rudder or elevator, which is rotated or moved by the pilot to change the attitude of the airplane.

control wheel: Controls the airplane in pitch, i.e., up and down.

controls: A control stick or control wheel actuated by hand, and left and right rudder pedals actuated by the feet. The controls move the control surfaces which in turn cause the plane to move about its three axes.

Cub, Piper: Originally the Taylor Cub; bought out by Piper. Most famous small plane of the 1930s-'40s. Initially 40 hp; later models have larger engines. Super Cub has 150 hp; some fitted with 180 hp to tow gliders.

DC-3, Douglas: 21-28 passenger low wing monoplane. Two 1,200 hp engines. First flight late in 1935. More than 10,000 military version (C-47) built for WWII. Surplus C-47s were used to establish many postwar airlines, including Ethiopian Airlines. A very famous airplane, nicknamed the Gooney Bird during WWII.

dope: A liquid brushed or sprayed on the airplane fabric covering before painting. Its purpose is to shrink the fabric drum-tight, and make it air- and water-tight.

drag: Air resistance resulting from aircraft structure passing through the air. Streamlining reduces the drag.

dual: A student's flight instruction. Flight instructor is pilot-in-command. Usually requires 6 to 12 hours minimum before soloing an airplane.

Eaglerock: In the 1920s and 1930s the Alexander Aircraft Company built the Alexander Eaglerock 3-seat (pilot and 2 passengers) biplane. Many of them were powered with the Curtiss OX5 engine.

elevator: The horizontal tail surface which makes the plane move about the pitch axis. The left elevator and right elevator usually are connected to each other. When the pilot pushes forward on the control wheel, the elevator trailing edge moves downward; the airstream strikes it, forcing the tail up and the nose down. Pulling back on the wheel causes the opposite reaction. If the improper loading of passengers or cargo results in a center of gravity that's too far forward or rearward, the pilot might not have enough elevator control movement to control the plane.

elevator rib: The truss-like part which is attached to the hinge tube running from the left hand elevator tip to the right hand elevator tip. On the B-17, the elevator ribs are spaced approximately one foot apart. Originally the fabric covering was hand-stitched to the elevator rib. Later, to reduce the labor required, U-shaped clips with barbs on the ends of the two legs were used to fasten the fabric to the elevator rib. The clips were then driven through the fabric and through holes drilled in the elevator rib. The legs sprang apart as they went through the rib, then sprang back together, holding the fabric securely in place.

elevator trim tab: A hinged tab on the trailing edge of the elevator which can be adjusted to trim the plane so it will fly "hands off," or to reduce the force on the control wheel required of the pilot to move the elevator.

emergency power: Maximum engine power rating for reciprocating engines, usually limited to 5 minutes. Used only in an actual emergency.

emergency procedure: A standard procedure determined to be the best course of action for the given emergency. Derived from the analysis of accident reports and/or from calculations.

engine requirement: Four 1200 hp Wright Cyclones on later model B-17s. Four 2200 hp Wright Double Cyclones on the B-29. Four 3500 hp Pratt & Whitney Wasp Majors on the B-50, C-97 and KC-97. Six 7,200 lb.-thrust GE 47's on the B-47E.

Experimental or Engineering Flight Test: This department performs flight R and D (research and development). Instrumentation for a particular test is installed over a one to three week period. The airplane is flight tested for one to three weeks, then laid up for instrumentation for the next test.

FAA: Federal Aeronautics Authority—the agency which governs civil aviation. Formerly entitled Civil Aviation Administration.

Fairchild 22: A 2-seat open cockpit parasol monoplane with a 90 hp Cirrus engine, built in the 1930s. The parasol wing is strut-braced, placed *above* the fuselage.

feather the propeller: Change the pitch of the propeller to align with the airstream flow, to stop the engine and decrease the drag of the propeller when the engine needs to be shut down.

ferry: To fly an aircraft without passengers/cargo, to deliver it to a customer or to a repair shop for repairs. A non-revenue flight.

flaps: Movable surfaces at the trailing edge of the wing that are controlled from the cockpit. They allow an airplane to fly slower and at a steeper angle during the landing approach. Partial flap settings shorten the takeoff roll on some airplanes.

flat pitch: On many airplanes, the propeller operates from zero degrees to ninety degrees pitch. At ninety degrees pitch the propeller is feathered, i.e., the leading edge of the propeller is forward in the direction of flight and the trailing edge of the propeller is directly behind in the direction of flight, to provide minimum drag when the engine is inoperative. Flat pitch is zero degrees pitch, the position assumed by the propeller when the throttles are closed. This position provides maximum drag, to slow the airplane on landing. On some airplanes, the propeller is moved to negative pitch and throttles are opened immediately upon landing, providing negative thrust to slow the airplane more rapidly. On rare occasions the propeller governor malfunctions in flight, causing the propeller to go into flat pitch. The engine then overspeeds because the propeller is in a no-load condition, i.e., it is not "biting" into the air.

Flight Engineer: The crew member who starts the engines, manages fuel flow, cabin heat, cabin pressure, and other functions.

Flight Test Engineer: Crew member who observes and records altitude, airspeed, temperatures, pressures and other phenomena during engineering test flights.

Flight Test, Engineering or Experimental: Flight research and development.

Flight Test, Production: Generally, pilots make a one to three hour flight operating the landing gear, flaps, spoilers, radios, navigation and other equipment to make sure all systems are operating and properly adjusted.

Ford Trimotor: A 14-seat high-wing all-metal airplane built in the 1930s, with three Wright Whirlwind 225 hp engines or Pratt & Whitney Wasp 420 hp engines. Nicknamed "Tin Goose," it carried cargo and was used to fight forest fires after becoming obsolete in passenger service.

Franklin PS-1 secondary glider: A fabric-covered welded-steel-tube framework, intermediate between open framework primary glider and high performance sailplane. Open cockpit, single wheel landing gear with skids on wing tips.

fuel tank vent: This system allows air to escape from the fuel tanks during climb, and to re-enter during descent. If the vent is too small, the tanks will collapse from external air pressure during descent. The vents also allow air to enter the tanks as fuel is used.

governor, propeller: Maintains constant rpm by varying the propeller pitch. Hydraulically actuated on B-17, B-29, et al. Electrically actuated on B-50.

hangar flying: To informally discuss flying, airplanes, pilots, and other aviation subjects. A hangar is a common site for such discussions. They frequently occur when weather is too poor for flying.

hp: Horsepower. See "emergency power." Emergency power is the maximum power which a reciprocating engine can develop.

Hudson Motor Co.: Built large Hudson and smaller Essex automobiles. Company went out of business in the 1930s.

hyperventilation: Rapid breathing. If hyperventilation at high altitude continues for only a few minutes, dizziness and then coma will result.

intercom: Intercommunication network (telephone) linking all crew stations.

knot: 1.15 mph. Early airplanes measured speed in miles per hour. Later planes measure speed in knots.

landing approach speed: The optimum airspeed for landing approach, fast enough to provide a safe margin above stall speed during the flare-out on landing, but slow enough to avoid excessive landing run.

leading edge: The foremost edge of an airfoil (wing or tail surface) or propeller blade.

Lincoln Standard L.S.5: 5 seat biplane in the 1920s with 180 hp Hisso (Hispano-Suiza) engine. Top speed 92 mph, landing speed approximately 35 mph.

magneto: The magneto generates a spark which ignites the fuel/air mixture in the engine cylinder.

maximum horsepower: See "hp."

mph: Miles per hour.

OX5, Curtiss: A famous 90 hp, 8 cylinder, water-cooled engine, built in quantity during WWI by the Curtiss company. This war surplus engine powered most of the 3-seat biplanes built during the 1920s and early 1930s.

photorecorder: A special instrument panel with a camera that photographs the panel at intervals (one second, ten seconds, etc.) to record instrument readings.

Piper Cub: A popular 2-seat taildragger, the J-2, J-3, Super Cub, etc. Can fly as slow as 47 mph. 9,000 built 1949-1980. 90, 125 and 150 hp versions. (See "Cub.")

placard speed: The maximum "Red Line" or not-to-be-exceeded speed for which the airplane was designed.

pressure mask: Required in unpressurized planes for flights above 35,000 feet. With a regular oxygen mask, crew member makes an effort to inhale oxygen, then relaxes to exhale. Above 35,000 feet the oxygen pressure is
turned up so that the breathing cycle is reversed: The crew member relaxes while the high pressure forces oxygen into the lungs; he then has to make a great effort to exhale against the high pressure.

Production Flight Test: See "flight test, production."

propeller governor: See "governor, propeller."

propeller noise: At high rpm the propeller noise is often greater than the engine exhaust noise because the propeller tips are moving faster than the speed of sound. This produces cavitation, which is pockets of vacuum on the front side of the propeller.

propping: Starting an airplane engine by turning the propeller by hand. A necessary procedure on early planes that had no starter. Careless pilots who've propped a plane without someone in the cockpit have had to jump out of the way when the engine started with the throttle open too far. Some pilotless planes have actually taken off. Careless pilots have been badly injured while propping.

puddle jumper: Nickname for any low-powered 1- or 2-seat plane such as a Cub.

receptacle, inflight refueling: The opening (located above the cockpit on the B-29 and B-50 receivers) into which the boom nozzle of the tanker is inserted to transfer fuel. It is V-shaped to guide the boom nozzle into the fuel intake plumbing.

ripcord: The cord which releases the pilot chute of a parachute. The pilot chute than opens and pulls the main canopy out of its container.

rpm: Revolutions per minute. The Curtiss OX5 engine turns 1400 rpm. The Wright R-3350 on the B-29 turns 2600. The Lycoming 150 hp engine on the Super Cub turns 2700. Jet engine turbines turn more than 10,000 rpm.

rudder pedals: The foot-actuated rudder pedals move the rudder.

ruddevators: The V-shaped tail surfaces on the end of the inflight refueling boom which are activated by the boom operator to control the motion of the boom. V-shaped tail also used on the famous Beech Bonanza airplane.

runway 25: On an airplane landing on runway 25, for example, the compass would read approximately 250 degrees, the heading of the runway.

"seat of the pants": Controlling an airplane by feel rather than by reference to instruments. Skids, slips, and other maneuvers are most noticeable in the pilot's seat.

shroud lines: Nylon cords connecting the parachute canopy with the parachute harness worn by the crew member. If they tangle, the chute won't open.

span: The distance from tip to tip of an airplane wing or tail surface.

spin: A maneuver with the nose of the airplane inclined steeply downward. The wing is stalled and the airplane rotates with a small radius. Also called "tailspin."

stabilizer: The fixed horizontal tail surface. The movable elevator is hinged to the trailing edge of the stabilizer. In some planes the forward edge of the stabilizer is adjustable up and down through a limited range to trim the plane for level flight.

stall: A term describing the condition of an airplane which has lost the forward speed necessary for flight and for control. Very dangerous when it occurs close to the ground, as it usually results in a fatal crash.

Stearman Aircraft Company: Founded in 1927 by Lloyd Stearman in Venice, California. Moved to Wichita, Kansas later in 1927. Reputation for stout airplanes. It became the Wichita Division of Boeing in the mid-1930s.

Stearman X-100: A high wing, twin engine light attack bomber. The first Stearman with an all-metal structure. The first flight, by Eddie Allen, was made in 1939. Only one prototype was built.

stenotypist: A court reporter type of reporter who records preflight and postflight conferences with a stenograph machine, rather than shorthand.

Stinson 10A: A 3-seat high wing monoplane, underpowered with an 80 hp engine. Superseding the 1920s biplanes, the Stinson and other airplanes had brakes, steerable tailwheel or tricycle gear, and self-starter.

sweptwing: A wing whose wingtips trail behind the point of attachment of the leading edge of the wing to the fuselage. The angle of sweepback on the B-47 is 35 degrees. Sweepback substantially increases airplane speed.

taildragger: Airplane which has a tailwheel instead of a nosewheel. More difficult to land than a nosewheel plane because it tends to groundloop, i.e., go out of control and make a rapid turn. Sometimes the wing tip is damaged by dragging on the ground, and the landing gear may be damaged.

tail-heavy: Rearward center of gravity. Condition in which the nose tends to rise if the control wheel is released. In this condition, recovering from a tailspin is difficult or impossible. Can be very dangerous.

tailspin: Same as "spin."

takeoff speed: "unstick speed," the speed at which the plane leaves the ground. On B-29 at 140,000 lbs. gross wt., 25 degrees flap, speed is 120 mph.

trimmed: Condition where plane flies level "hands off," neither climbs nor descends, when trim tab or horizontal stabilizer is properly adjusted.

trim tab: A control surface on the trailing edge of the control surfaces which can be moved to trim the plane for straight and level flight "hands off."

Wright R-3350 engine: Used on the B-29. 2200 hp at 2600 rpm, 47.5 inches Hg (mercury) manifold pressure, and 290 gallons fuel per hour.

zoom: To climb for a short time at an angle greater than that which can be sustained in steady flight, the aircraft being carried upward at the expense of its kinetic energy. This term is sometimes used as a noun, to denote any sudden increase in the upward slope of the flight path.

Photo Credits